Modern world issues

Series editor: John Turner

Only a game?

Sport in the modern world

Tony Mason

Reader in Social History, Centre for the Study of Social History
University of Warwick

CAMBRIDGE
UNIVERSITY PRESS

Published by the Press Syndicate of the University of Cambridge
The Pitt Building, Trumpington Street, Cambridge CB2 1RP
40 West 20th Street, New York, NY 10011–4211, USA
10 Stamford Road, Oakleigh, Victoria 3166, Australia

© Cambridge University Press 1993

First published 1993

Printed in Great Britain by Scotprint Limited,
Musselburgh

A catalogue record for this book is available from the
British Library
ISBN 0 521 39992 0 paperback

Illustrations by Amanda MacPhail

Acknowledgements

The author and publisher would like to thank the
following for permission to reproduce copyright
material:

Front cover: The final of the 1991 Barcelona GP.
Gray Mortimore / Allsport UK Ltd.

5t, Catherine Ashmore; 5b, Norton/Bob Thomas Sports
Photography; 6, 7t, 46, Hulton-Deutsch Collection; 7b,
57, Gary Mortimore / Allsport; 9, Joyner / Bob Thomas
Sports Photography; 11, The Boston Herald / The
Picture Cube; 13t, 21, 27, 39, 40, 55, Bob Thomas
Sports Photography; 13b, Tempsport / Bob Thomas
Sports Photography; 17, 66, Tony Duffy / Allsport; 18,
F.G. / Allsport; 19, 32, Sally & Richard Greenhill; 20,
David Cannon / Allsport; 22, 25, Colorsport; 26, Bob
Martin / Allsport; 29, courtesy of Mars Confectionery;
33, Rex Features; 34, Collections of Alex cartoon strips
published by Penguin; 36, Sporting Pictures (UK) Ltd;
37, Allsport; 47, Associated Press; 50, George P.
Herringshaw / Associated Sports Photography; 53, 76,
Adrian Murrell / Allsport; 54, Francois Lochon / Frank
Spooner Pictures; 64, Steve Powell / Allsport; 68, J-Y
Ruszniewski / Bob Thomas Sports Photography; 69,
Ed Lacey / Associated Sports Photography; 70,
reproduced by permission of Punch; 73, Popperfoto; 77,
Gerry Cranham.

Every effort has been made to reach copyright holders;
the publisher would be glad to hear from anyone
whose rights they have unwittingly infringed.

Contents

Opening up the issues

What is sport? The Sports Council in Britain ought to know: they tell us that it is a physical activity which provides an acceptable balance of play, effort and skill.

Members of the English National Ballet performing Coppelia.

A game of American football between the London Monarchs and the Barcelona Dragons. Footballers and ballet dancers share many athletic skills. Are the differences between them greater than their similarities?

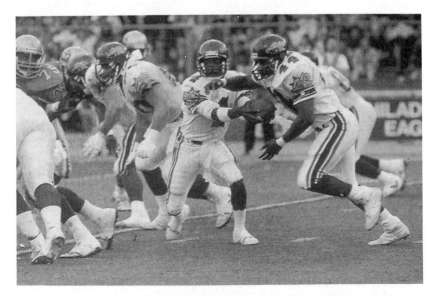

So is ballet a sport? Many people would probably deny it. Sport is certainly a pleasure of the flesh. For many it is a recreational activity. There is usually an element of competition. There will probably be an organisational framework: clubs, leagues, associations. Sport obviously has several levels, from the casual games of street and park, to organised participation on a regular basis, up to the spectacular performances staged at stadiums in every country in the world.

Sport has existed historically in most countries worldwide. But the sports which have captured the attention of the modern world were invented in the growing industrial and urban nations of the West in the nineteenth century, especially the United States and Britain.

The legacy of the British public school

In many respects, modern sport was refined and organised in the nineteenth-century British public school. Certainly athletics, boxing, cricket, football (soccer), hockey, some racquet sports, rowing and rugby were developed there. The schoolmasters who were responsible had ulterior motives. They wanted to keep adolescent boys in control during those turbulent teenage years. Organised sport might direct youthful energy. But they also wanted to make men of them. Sport was aimed at toughening the body but also at building character so that the graduate of the public school could go forth and lead both nation and British Empire. Character was to be constructed by learning to control the temper and sexual desire. It was also necessary to learn how to lose, and how to promote qualities like fairness and honour.

Sport in the British public school: sport was not only something to be enjoyed – it was seen as an activity which could improve and shape the character of those who participated.

Restrictive clothing: early twentieth-century fashions and conventions dictated that women should wear clothes which prevented easy movement as this picture of a Danish gymnast performing the high jump at the 1908 Olympics shows. Fabrics and fashions had changed greatly by 1989 when Jamaican athlete Merlene Ottey won the 100 metres at Budapest.

But sport was essentially for men. Women were to be merely their mothers and wives. The fact that only women could give birth to the next generation was thought to be the determining factor in their lives. Vital organs would be damaged by athletic activity. Playing sport would not only encourage masculine qualities of aggression and competitiveness but also produce muscular women who looked more like men.

For many years doctors discouraged physical exertion by women. So did the clothes which fashion and convention dictated women must wear. By 1914 some women with both time and money had rebelled against these ideas.

This rebellion was part of a wider movement for women's rights which saw, for example, an expansion of secondary and further education.

It reflected a gradual shift in medical opinion towards the view that the health of women might be improved by more exercise. But men's and women's sports were strictly segregated, and women were also limited to those sports which society thought appropriate. They might play croquet, golf and tennis and they might swim, but running, throwing, boxing, football and cricket were forbidden territory. It would be well into the twentieth century before male – and female – attitudes to women's sport began to change.

Fair play

The aim of the public schools was to produce an elite of leaders from the aristocracy and the middle class who would share both an education and a view of the world. Team sports were especially valued for their contribution to group loyalty. Those who played together stayed together. Games were to be compulsory in the public schools until well into the twentieth century. The key phrase was 'fair play'. It was important to stick to the rules but also to observe the spirit of the game. In theory, gentlemen should not need a referee because they would not infringe either the laws of the game or its spirit.

The public school sportsmen did their missionary work too well. Their sports became popular outside the ranks of educated gentlemen. The popularity of sport rapidly led to its commercialisation in the three decades after 1870. Modern patterns of sport had emerged in both Britain and the United States by 1900. The presence of money enhanced the importance of winning and undermined the virtue of fair play. British sport became divided between gentlemen amateurs who would not play for pay, and working-class professionals who could not play without it. The partisanship of the crowds also mocked the idea of fair play. But sport proved attractive to men in all social classes. Masculine qualities like strength, courage and skill were thought to be encouraged by it. It created emotional and social bonds between them. It became an inheritance which one generation bequeathed to the next.

A British export

Because of Britain's special position in the late nineteenth century – leading manufacturer, banker, trader and centre of the Empire – sport was exported, with British goods and services, around the world. The new sports penetrated Europe and South America as well

An advertisement for probably the first football match in Norway, 1886.

as Australia, Africa and India. Only the United States resisted successfully. Even there, baseball and football were adapted from British models: only basketball was a truly American invention. Britain was admired, feared and emulated.

School cricket in the West Indies.

The famous English cricketer, W. G. Grace, on the Australian bicentenary postage stamp, 1988.

It seems that once particular sports become established in a country, they are not easily replaced by newcomers. True, the balance of popularity between different sports shifts over time, but the most popular sports in 1900 are still the most popular today.

Football in particular was taken up just about everywhere in the world by 1920. What is particularly interesting about this essentially British export, though, is that the style of playing soon began to vary from one country to another. By the 1930s, international football had developed into a clash of styles, with the stamina, speed and finishing power of the British set against the superior ball control and more careful approach of other Europeans and South Americans.

The issues

The eight chapters which follow isolate some of the key questions raised by sport in the modern world.

Chapter one asks which sports are played for fun, by whom and why? Do some groups play more than others? Are some countries more enthusiastic about sport than others?

The second chapter looks at sport as a career. Would you want your child to be a professional sports player? The chapter looks at three case studies: English football, Kenyan athletics and Japanese baseball.

Chapter three asks why the relationship between sport and business has become so close worldwide. What do the sponsors of sport get in return for their money? Are there dangers in the marriage of business and sport?

The fourth chapter considers why spectators stand on the terraces, sit around the boxing ring or look on from the track side. It also explores the place of television in modern sport.

Chapter five looks at how sport is used for political purposes by ethnic minority groups, political parties or governments. These points are illustrated by looking in some detail at the place of sport in East–West relations and its role in the struggle over South Africa. Can sport avoid being used for nationalist ends?

The search for physical perfection and psychological fitness has brought science into sport in almost as big a way as it has brought business into it. As chapter six shows, the gains are obvious, but are there losses too?

Chapter seven looks at the place of performance-enhancing drugs in sport. Who uses them and why? Can drugs ever be considered fair play?

Chapter eight shows that Sport for All does not quite mean what it appears to mean. Sport can obviously damage your physical health and competitive pressure can, at the very least, place a strain on players' integrity. But there is a wonderful quality to sport which enhances the lives of those who are touched by it. It is an international language though not everyone speaks it.

1 Playing for fun

Why play sport?

It is often proclaimed by people in Britain that the purpose of playing any sport ought to be for fun. Look up the word fun in a dictionary and you will find that it means diversion, sport, boisterous gaiety. If anything is 'done in fun' it is either meant as a joke or at least not to be taken seriously. But for lots of people, part of the fun of playing sport is the seriousness with which they take it. Even the casual games of football and cricket that are still a feature of many parks and other public open spaces can be taken very seriously indeed.

People play sport for different reasons. Fun and enjoyment is likely to be one of them, but there may be others. You may play sport because your friends do; you may join a sports club in order to make friends or to meet members of the opposite sex. Tennis and badminton, for example, are played by both men and women; that may be a sufficient reason to attract some people to those sports. Badminton is on the menu of most leisure centres. In Britain, six times as many players played badminton as watched League football in 1988.

The Boston marathon, which first took place at the end of the nineteenth century, did not admit women until 1972. When Kathy Switzer entered in 1967 attempts were made to evict her from the race. Today, most marathons receive many more entries than can be accommodated as participants.

There are other reasons for taking up a particular sport. Joining the local golf club may provide business contacts or recognition that you have reached a certain eminence in the local community. Success in sport – at whatever level – tends to enhance the status of those who achieve it.

Active sportsmen and women often say that they do what they do in order to feel fit. Swimming, running, even squash, are not always engaged in for the opportunities they provide to compete against other players. Jogging and swimming can be done alone. Apart from access to a pool, neither of these sports demands much in the way of facilities or well-developed physical skills.

That cannot be said for all sport. You cannot just take part in a marathon, for example. To run 26 miles, you have to prepare your body by regular training, which takes a lot of time and a lot of effort. Why do people do it?

Perhaps it has something to do with the challenge of the distance and the effort required to run it. It is a triumph just to finish a marathon, although improving the time it takes is also important to some runners. Perhaps it has something to do with the fact that strenuous physical exercise apparently produces a kind of euphoria or excitement in some people.

Sport at school

Playing sport is mainly for the young. But this is less true today than it once was. Many of those sports in which numbers participating have expanded most in the last decade in Britain – badminton, bowls, golf, running and swimming – are practised by the over-45s.

Most people in post-1945 Britain were probably introduced to organised sport at school. This was not always the case. In 1890, for example, Physical Education in all the schools in continental Europe was based on non-competitive exercises. Only in the British public schools and grammar schools were competitive sports, and especially the team games of cricket, football, hockey and rugby, dominant; and only a very small proportion of young people attended these schools.

In the 1990s, however, despite a growing enthusiasm for movement education and the introduction of a much greater variety of recreative activities in schools, physical education in Britain and many other countries is still dominated by competitive sport. This has been good for those who have liked the dominant sports or played them to a reasonable standard. But for those who found sport unattractive, its compulsory nature – in British state schools since the 1944 Education Act – often made 'games' lessons a miserable experience. Sport was certainly not fun for them.

Sport can be encouraged in the home or promoted by the voluntary sports club, but school is an important sporting institution. In the last decade there has been much anxiety expressed by sports administrators and politicians in Britain that school sport has lost both resources and prestige. In 1987 a working party set up by the Secondary Schools Heads Association asked how sport was managing in over 5,000 secondary schools containing over four million pupils. Since 1985, 95 per cent of schools reported a decline in school fixtures, 70 per cent claimed inadequate playing fields and indoor facilities, with 75 per cent of pupils having no opportunity to learn to swim at school. Pupils aged between 12 and 14 had an average of two hours physical exercise per week; 65 per cent of all

Should sport be competitive? Women playing lacrosse in an international match between England and Scotland in 1987.

Aerobics – a non-competitive sport – has become a popular method of keeping fit.

16–19-year-olds were allowed to opt out of Physical Education. Nearly half of all playing fields were sub-standard. Such a situation was made worse by government cuts in public spending, with pressure on local education authorities to follow suit. Falling school rolls were used as an excuse to sell off school playing fields for development. At the same time, increased workloads for teachers made it more difficult for them to supervise out-of-school sports activities.

Encouraging participation

On the positive side, there are some interesting recent initiatives. The Football Association, for example, keen to remedy what it claims as a 60–70 per cent decline in the time spent teaching football skills in schools, has set up coaching centres for boys and girls aged 8–13. Courses last six weeks, with one hour per week devoted to technique – ball familiarity, ball control, passing, dribbling, shooting and heading.

A number of small-scale variations of sports have been developed to encourage schoolchildren to participate actively. Short tennis, for example, was introduced from Sweden in the early 1980s and now involves over 200,000 child players in Britain.

The Amateur Athletics Association began its Ten Step Award scheme in 1985. Aimed at 8–10 year olds, it comprised nineteen activities based on the four basics of running, jumping, skipping and throwing. Points were awarded for reaching specified standards in each activity. The scheme is an attempt to get away from one of the most persistent criticisms levelled at school sport – that it chose the best and left the rest – as it was open to all, irrespective of ability. Children were also encouraged to measure and record the efforts of their classmates. Supporters of the scheme emphasised its value in teaching fairness and honesty as well as athletic skills.

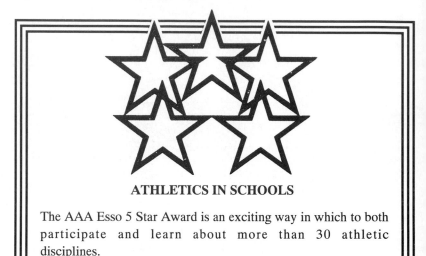

ATHLETICS IN SCHOOLS

The AAA Esso 5 Star Award is an exciting way in which to both participate and learn about more than 30 athletic disciplines.

The 5 Star Proficiency Scheme is aimed at young athletes and helps to improve their performance by the use of graded scoring tables split into various age groups. The young athlete is able to gain a series of badges and certificates depending on his or her proficiency.

The 1,2,3,4 and the coveted 5 Star Awards are achievable in track, field and cross country events. Pentathlon and Decathlon awards are also available across a range of events to suit the young athlete.

The scheme, developed by the Amateur Athletic Association over a decade ago, has been instrumental in helping to produce many of the country's top athletes of today.

The scheme is run by schools on behalf of the AAA and certificates and badges are available from the school, who hold all the necessary scoring tables and instructions and make arrangements for pupils to take part in 5 Star activities.

In some respects, schemes such as the Amateur Athletics Association Ten Step Award are reminiscent of the proficiency and badge system that was started in the Soviet Union in 1931 and has been revised several times since. These programmes were aimed at adults as well as children. By 1964, for example, Russian men aged between 19 and 39 had to be able to climb 4 metres up a rope or pole; run 100 metres in 14 seconds; run 1,500 metres in 5 minutes and 30 seconds; long jump 4.3 metres; hurl a 700-gram grenade 35 metres; swim 100 metres in 2 minutes 30 seconds; ski 10 kilometres in 1 hour 5 minutes; and score a certain number of points firing a small-bore rifle at 50 metres. As they also had to perform eight moving exercises satisfactorily and answer questions on first aid, sport and hygiene, it was quite a test. Clearly the goal was the physical fitness of the population for the purposes of national defence. It has never been clear how many men reached these impressive standards.

Who takes part?

Comparing rates of participation in sports across national boundaries is very difficult. The methods of collecting statistics are far from uniform, and definitions of participation far from agreed. But in Western Europe by the 1970s, it was clear that after leaving school, participation in sport was low among women, ethnic minorities, the unemployed, the low paid and the elderly. Income, lifestyle and social environment were obviously factors in who played sport. Sport was largely male, young and, as often as not, a province of the better-off.

There is some evidence to suggest that the situation was different in those countries where the state invested large sums of money in sports facilities, coaching and the scientific study of sport. In the Soviet Union, East Germany and Cuba, for example, such investment produced a rich dividend in elite sporting success, most notably at the Olympics and the world championships in athletics, boxing, gymnastics and rowing. In the 1976 Olympics, East Germany won 40 gold medals while the United States won only 34, despite having almost 200,000,000 more people. Of the East German population 16 per cent were said to be members of sports clubs, as opposed to about eleven per cent in Britain and perhaps ten per cent in the USA. Sport was not just for the few but was a way of creating a fit and healthy population. Certainly more women seemed to take part in regular sport in East Germany than in Britain and the USA.

However, since the dramatic political changes in Europe in 1989, with the collapse of Communist regimes throughout the Eastern bloc, doubt has been cast on the high levels of participation in sport claimed for the countries of Eastern Europe and Cuba. It is now suggested that most ordinary sporting facilities were as shabby and inadequate as almost everything else behind the Wall!

There is an amusing saying about sport: it is not worth playing if it is not worth playing badly. Many people would like to be sporting stars, but the vast majority of players learn – usually very quickly – that they will never attain such eminence. But that does not mean that they cannot enjoy their chosen sport at their own particular level.

Playing for fun means playing because you want to, not because the government insists that you should. When a group of people were asked, in the late 1960s, to place in order of importance five attractions of taking part in sport, pleasure of competition was placed

Advertisement in the Birmingham Sports Argus.

last by women, and next-to-last by men. The chance to mix with other people, to forget about other things for a while and to get out into the open air were way ahead. Playing sport is part of the way people make friends and share experiences.

These attitudes have been reflected in the shift away from competitive sport in schools. Education should involve physical as well as mental development. Children need to know how the body works and what needs to be done to keep it in trim. This might produce an emphasis on personal achievement at the expense of competition. Ideally, children should be able to choose from a wide range of physical activities. This does not mean the end of competitive sport in schools, but it may mean a realignment of its dominant – some would say overdominant – position.

New attitudes to sport and leisure

More people are playing sport for fun in more countries than ever before. About 6.3 million people were members of sporting organisations in Britain in 1983. About 48.5 million were not, but many of them may have been irregular sporting participants. Throughout Europe and North America, the gradual expansion of leisure time, an increase in disposable income, and a growing awareness that good health can be aided by regular exercise, has encouraged more and more people to take part in sport. Considerable investment has been made in sports and leisure centres. Even hotels often point to a gymnasium as an added attraction.

In Britain, many of these sporting facilities have been traditionally paid for out of local taxation. It remains to be seen what the effect on popular participation will be of the British government's decision to privatise local authority leisure facilities. Should sports facilities be subject to the working of the free market? Or should sports centres and swimming baths be subsidised for wider social reasons? Even playing for fun cannot escape politics.

2 Playing for money

Hitting the big time

Most people who play sport are not aiming to make money. However, for a talented minority, there has never been greater opportunity to make what, to ordinary workers, seem like fantastic sums. In boxing or marathon running, football or baseball, tennis, golf or snooker, there seems no end to the flow of money. It comes not only from prizes and salaries, but also from commercial sponsorship and the endorsement by sportsplayers of the products of particular companies. The amount of money available is further increased by worldwide television coverage.

Leading British athletes of recent years such as Sebastian Coe and Steve Cram could reckon on appearance money of £10–20,000 each time they raced.

Some individual examples emphasise the point. World snooker champion, Steve Davis, was thought to be receiving more than £1 million per year in 1984, but 80 per cent of it was earned away from the table. When Scottish golfer, Sandy Lyle, won the Open Golf Championship, he immediately signed a contract with Mizumo Golf Clubs of Japan worth £40,000 over three years, and other similarly remunerative deals with Adidas and Ballantines Whisky. He did not have to do very much. It was mainly a matter of allowing his name to be used in advertising products and being present at various promotional events. The Czech tennis player, Ivan Lendl, had won over $13 million in prize money by 1989 and the Kenyan marathon champion, Douglas Wakiihuri, was offered £88,397 simply to run in the 1990 London Marathon. A Scottish Sunday newspaper revealed the salaries of the footballers of Celtic and Rangers for the season 1988/89. This showed that the Rangers' goalkeeper earned more than all but two of the highest-paid Scottish businessmen. Almost all leading sportsplayers have agents who will charge a fee for virtually anything their employer is asked to do – from appearances to interviews.

Who should earn more? Heavy-weight boxers are traditionally among the highest paid sportspeople in the world. In November 1991, for example, American champion heavyweight Mike Tyson shared a prize of $15 million for a single fight.

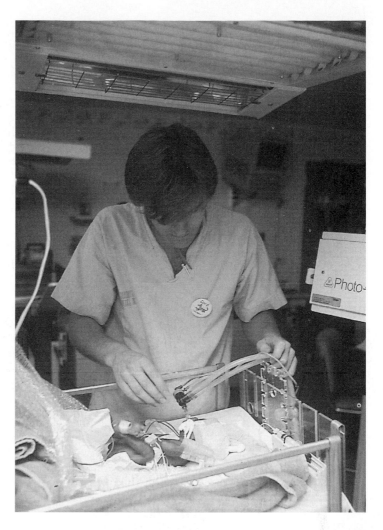

Special skills: a nurse cares for a premature baby.

Some people think that such large earnings for sports personalities are out of all proportion to their contribution to society. Are they as socially useful as nurses, teachers, electricity workers, agricultural labourers or scientists? Others argue that well-known sports personalities are part of the entertainment industry and that other members of that industry have long earned large sums of money. Why should there be a different rule for sports personalities? They have a special talent, which large numbers of other people want to see displayed. It deserves the highest reward which the market is prepared to offer.

It is also often said that a career in sport is short. Few sportsmen and sportswomen survive for more than a few years at the top, and they often have to give up just when other people's careers are taking off. A career in sport is also risky. It might be brought to an end at any time by injury or loss of form. Moreover, it is unfair to concentrate on the high earnings of the few. Most professional sportsplayers earn far less than the highly paid minority. In 1987, for example, 12 snooker players each earned over £100,000 in prize money, and 20 more players pocketed over £20,000. However, the bottom 65 players out of the 128 tournament professionals only received £7,000 each in prize money. Their opportunities for outside earnings were also, of course, correspondingly less. In professional football, too, earnings vary considerably. Many footballers cannot match the salaries offered by Celtic and Rangers.

Professional sport has offered a way out of anonymous poverty for working-class males in many Western countries for most of this century. Some Africans and Asians are now being offered similar opportunities. In theory, sport offers a fair chance to all. Class, race and religion – but not gender – are less important in sport than talent. Everyone is equal within the rules of the game.

What pathway to the stars might an aspiring champion follow? Let us look at three different sports in three different parts of the world – football in England, middle-distance running in Kenya and baseball in Japan – and examine how players can become professionals.

Football in England: a case study

Football (soccer) remains one of the most popular sports for young men throughout the world. FIFA, the sport's world governing body, has more member countries than the United Nations. Football is easy to play, has simple rules and does not demand expensive facilities. In England, most young boys play football in secondary school. The best players are selected for the school team, and the best eleven from a particular locality are chosen to represent all the schools in that area. There are some 270 teams in the English Schools Football Association, and the 3,000 boys who play for them are the 14–15 year-old elite of their generation. Scouts from professional clubs watch all of these young footballers play and by 14 most of them will have signed an associated schoolboy form, which allows a professional club to train and coach them. If they are considered good enough, the next stage could be to sign as an apprentice footballer at 16, the school-leaving age.

In 1984, the British government, as part of its Youth Training Scheme (YTS), began to subsidise a one-year, and from 1986 a two-year, training course for school leavers who wanted to make a career in professional football. It was a way of persuading clubs to take on more young players and reduce the number of the young unemployed. At any one time, a thousand young men were learning the game.

Another recent innovation, set up by the Football Association in 1984 and sponsored by General Motors until 1990, is the National School at Lilleshall in Shropshire. It is a football boarding school which boys stay at between the ages of 14 and 16. They play football for one and a half hours each day and attend a nearby secondary school for other school lessons. Boys can apply for one of the twenty or so places available each year. Most of those who do have attended one of the many regional centres, usually linked to a professional club, where about 5,000 11–14-year-olds have weekly coaching sessions.

Many English professional footballers will have gone through the school, the apprentice or the YTS system. But there is also a plethora of amateur and semi-professional football leagues which offer a path towards a career in the paid elite. Professional football often provides a career for talented working-class boys and the rewards – of money, fame and glory – are great for those who can attain them.

A young footballer cleans the balls at the football boarding school in Lilleshall, Shropshire.

Leading English footballer Paul Gascoigne, who signed to play with the Italian team, Lazio, in 1992: his career is a classic example of the opportunities – and dangers – open to extremely talented footballers from working-class backgrounds. They can command as much media attention for their exploits off as on the field.

Middle-distance running in Kenya: a case study

Football is the most popular sport in Kenya too, but it is not football which has put Kenya on the sporting map of the world. It is athletics, and in particular the achievements of male middle-distance runners in all the distances between 800 metres and the marathon. Eight medals were won in the Olympics of 1968, six in 1972, two in 1984 and seven in 1988. Kenya took part in the boycotts of the Olympic Games in 1976 and 1980. The winners of all 45 of Kenya's Olympic and Commonwealth Games medals between 1963 and 1975 came from only two of the country's thirty or so tribal groups. At the Olympics in Seoul in 1988, nine of the Kenyan athletes had been to the same secondary school.

This concentration of athletes in a relatively small area in the west of the country which contains only 15 per cent of Kenya's total population, is not easy to explain! It is true the athletes grew up living at 6,000–8,000 feet (1,800–2,400 metres) above sea level and

(Right) *Kip Keino of Kenya at the Munich Olympics in 1972.*

(Below) *Paul Ereng of Kenya winning the 800 metres final at the Seoul Olympics in 1988.*

so their hearts and lungs were adapted to less oxygen in the atmosphere. It is also the case that in their rural society many young men did a lot of running up and down hills after cattle and goats and, more recently, some ran to and from school. The people from that area also have a high-protein diet. However, other peoples have similar lifestyles and have not produced such a series of champions. What other factors might have operated in the Kenyan case?

Athletics was introduced into Kenya by the British administrators of the colony before the Second World War. It was partly aimed at providing something prestigious for young warriors to do, in the hope that it would stop them rustling other people's cattle. Soon a regional system of athletic championships was set up throughout the whole of British East Africa. These culminated in three national championships and, starting in the 1950s, an East African championship. Prizes of useful goods were often awarded to the winners.

Athletic achievement became an important qualification for a secure job in the police, prison service or the army, especially after Kenya became independent in 1963. In a rapidly changing society, a regular cash income was a big attraction, and athletic prowess opened the door to it. Members of Kenya's running tribes are vastly over-represented in both the army and the police. Moreover, rivalry between these two services has led them both to seek out good runners and to provide them with the time and opportunity to train and compete.

Even some schools now offer inducements to promising child athletes. Primary schools can allow outstanding runners to stay on an extra year in order to have a better chance of passing the highly competitive examination which qualifies them for secondary school. Teacher training colleges recruit athletes from secondary schools, and American universities have been offering scholarships to Kenyan athletes for the last twenty years. Television has made athletics more visible and, as more and more Kenyans compete abroad, the attractions of foreign travel, free equipment and appearance money have grown.

The Kisii and the Kalenjin tribes have dominated running at every level. They expect to do well and the rest of the population expect them to do well too. A powerful tradition has been developed. Two generations of superathletes have provided role models for those coming after. But this only applies to the men. The idea that the place of Kenyan women is in the home, and not on the running track, is still very powerful.

Baseball in Japan: a case study

Athletes in Kenya have largely been drawn from a rural society. Career footballers in England have mainly been produced by urban environments, increasingly Merseyside and London. Baseball is the national sport of Japan and, like football in England, is largely an urban phenomenon.

Baseball has been a professional sport in Japan since 1934. Its popularity even enabled it to survive the nationalist prohibition of other Western sports in the late 1930s. Most professional players will have graduated via the high-school or college game – baseball is an important part of life in many Japanese high schools. A nationwide high-school knock-out competition has been held since 1915. Ten teams took part in that year. Now, almost 4,000 take part in what television has helped to make one of the highlights of the Japanese sporting year. A series of regional competitions reduces the 4,000

Victory parade at Hiroshima, following the tournament in 1957. This was the first local victory since the war, and helped to lift morale after the dropping of the atomic bomb.

23

down to 49, and for two weeks in August, at the Koshien stadium near Osaka, the top schoolboy teams in the country battle for supremacy. Many high schools scout the junior high schools for promising players.

Singing the school song, after a tournament match.

A mere appearance at the Koshien tournament can lead to the offer of a professional contract, not to mention instant fame and, in Japan, respect for a lifetime. It can also smooth the entrance to one of Japan's leading universities – like being good at cricket or rugby *used* to gain privileged access to Cambridge and Oxford. Even if no professional contract is offered or wanted, appearance at Koshien – like an Oxbridge 'blue' – can lead to the offer of a good job.

Over half the professional baseball players in Japan were and are recruited at the National High School Baseball Tournament. Professional teams also look at university players and those in the semi-professional leagues, but if you have ambitions to play 'pro-ball' in Japan it is a great advantage to have attended one of the top baseball high schools such as P. L. Gakuen, in southern Osaka.

This school was only founded in 1954 but it has competed at Koshien 25 times and has already won the title on 6 occasions, which is more than anyone else. It has 800 pupils and a carefully chosen baseball squad of 60, of whom only 15 can play for the first team. Such schools are sometimes criticised for selecting students for their baseball skills and subsequently allowing them to neglect their academic work. On the other hand, their concentration and discipline is thought to make them the world's best players for their age.

These three case studies show the importance of an early start on the road to a playing career in professional sport. They also underline the importance of institutions – schools, colleges, army, police – in providing the time and resources to practise and compete. But there are many pitfalls awaiting the young sportsplayers as they begin a process that perhaps they, and their parents, hope will lead to stardom.

Only 2 per cent of all eligible college American football and basketball players ever reach the professional ranks.

Pitfalls for the professional

Many are called but few chosen
Of the 200 boys who used to join English football league clubs each year as apprentices, 75 per cent were discarded by the age of 21. It will be interesting to see if the graduates of the Football Association school do any better.

25

The Soviet gymnast, Elena Chouchounova, performing at the Seoul Olympics in 1988, where she won the individual gold medal. Do young performers who undertake heavy training regimes before and during adolescence, suffer serious long-term physical damage?

Such warnings are underlined by the results of research in the USA. Only 600 major-league baseball players manage an average career of seven years. The average career span in the National Football League is only four years.

The physical pressures are enormous

Many good athletes find it difficult to cope with the physical pressures, especially the training, and in some sports that training can come very early. Ten-year-old swimmers, for example, may be doing 20 hours training a week.

Family lives have to be structured around training schedules. The Soviet gymnast, Elena Chouchounova, who won the individual gold medal in the women's gymnastics at the Seoul Olympics in 1988, said afterwards that she trained between eight and twelve hours a day and had done so since the age of six. Such pressures can put a strain on young frames. In 1987, the Great Ormond Street Hospital for Children in London tested 520 young gymnasts. They suggested that two-thirds could develop permanent back injuries within ten years.

There can be psychological problems
Parents sometimes look to their children to fulfil their own unrealised sporting ambitions. This can lead to bullying if the children fail to come up to expectations. There have been suggestions in several countries that children under 14 should not specialise in only one sport. The Sports Council in Britain has begun a research project on the training of young athletes in which it will try to monitor both the benefits and the harmful effects of child sport.

A young rugby player receives treatment for an injury on the pitch. Early achievement can bring success and greater maturity; it can also bring psychological pressure, and a disrupted family, school and social life.

A short career?

Top-level sport is very visible in modern society. Television means that World Cup football, for example, can be seen not only on the ground in Rome, but also in Sicilian villages, Medellin suburbs, remote Indian rural districts and African townships. Compared to many of the young viewers, professional sportsplayers live well-fed, well-housed and glamorous lives. It is bound to appear a highly desirable if barely reachable option.

However, it would be sensible to advise players everywhere to make sure of their educational qualifications before embarking on a career in professional sport. In England the FA claims such advice is embedded in its code of practice. But when you have signed for Manchester United the temptations to forget about education are difficult to resist! Nevertheless, British tennis player Sarah Loosemore seems to have made a wise choice. She comes from a family of tennis players and has had maximum opportunity and encouragement to play. She chose to do A level examinations, and has obtained a deferred university entrance while she tries to become a successful professional tennis player.

Education and sports can be combined via sports scholarships. These have not been traditional in Britain and only four universities awarded them in 1988. In the USA, of course, this has been one of the most popular routes to a professional career. A recent calculation showed that over 500 colleges offered scholarships in football alone. But such scholarships have often been concealed professionalism, with the holders of the awards receiving very little in the way of education, or being granted degrees for which they had not worked. Failure to make the sporting grade left many young men – often black – with no job and no higher education.

Finally, the sportsman or sportswoman who has built a successful career still has the problem of what to do when the cheering stops at 30, 35 or perhaps 40. Sport is big business almost everywhere. There are more jobs in its administration than ever before. But many old pros say nothing beats playing and they never adjust to a life without it.

Jenny Turrall: between 1974 and 1976 the young and waif-like swimming champion broke the 1500 metres freestyle record a total of five times. But she grew up. Though the favourite for the 800 metres gold medal at the Montreal Olympics in 1976, Jenny Turrall put on weight before the Games and finished last in the final. Soon after returning to Australia she retired – at the age of 16.

Blocking the urges of growth, pain, hunger and ...yes, sex too

• Jenny Turrall broke the world 1,500 metres freestyle record when she was 13, a slip of a girl at 5ft 2in and 6st 12lb. Six months later she weighs nearly a stone more and she's two inches taller.

World championship swimming is dynamics and dedication. Jenny can sustain the dedication but how long can she control the dynamics? Just as long as her coach can make her play Peter Pan and never grow up, it seems.

Her coach is Forbes Carlile who, with his wife, runs the world's biggest swimming school near Sydney. The secret, he says, is keeping puberty at bay. 'The proportion of body weight to muscle begins to fall off at puberty. We try to hold them back. This is an area of sacrifice: we allow no empty calories, no cakes, no biscuits, no sweets.'

Carlile's swimmers are on no freak diets, though. They don't even count calories. They are simply encouraged to eat plenty of beef, fish, eggs, fruit and vegetables.

Every day they put Jenny on the scales. 'We begrudge her every pound. It is essential she remains lean.' But you can't resist nature for ever. Jenny, like all swimming nymphets, *will* eventually grow up.

1974

3 Sports business

An independent Olympics?

In 1948 the Olympic Games was held in London. Several companies offered their products to the British team. Some even asked for some form of public recognition of their generosity. The British Olympic Association (BOA), which was determined to avoid any whiff of commercialism or professionalism, drew up a short, sharp set of rules:

> • no product could be described as 'Olympic'
> • no donor could use the name or photograph of a competitor in any advertisement, nor suggest that any gift made to the team had contributed to victory
> • all a company could say was that they had supplied items for use at the Olympics

Advertisement in a British national newspaper, 1988, prior to the Seoul Olympics.

The BOA did, however, accept free cartons of a milk drink, Horlicks, for the British team. That was 1948. Things were very different at the Seoul Olympics in 1988.

With the help of the German sports goods company, Adidas, and its subsidiary company, International Sport and Leisure, the International Olympic Committee (IOC) set up commercial sponsorship of the Games on a global basis. This was known as TOP – The Olympic Programme. In return for undisclosed sums, nine multinational companies were given exclusive world rights to use the Olympic name and five-ring logo on a range of their products.

The companies involved in the TOP programme
  Coca-Cola (soft drinks)
  Kodak (photographic products and services)
  Federal Express (fast delivery services)
  Visa (credit cards and traveller's cheques)
  3M (products ranging from thermal insulation to Scotch tape)
  Time Inc (international publishing)
  Brother (typewriters and office equipment)
  Philips (television monitors and audio equipment)
  Matsushita Electronic (video equipment)

How had such a change come about in forty years?

• The growth in the size and grandeur of the Olympic Games meant that it had become formidably expensive to put on. The city of Montreal had almost gone bankrupt in staging the 1976 Olympics. Governments subsequently became reluctant to saddle tax payers with such a financial burden.
• The attempts by some countries to boycott the Games of 1980 and 1984 suggested that relying on governments could threaten IOC control of the Games.

Professional sportsplayer

A professional sportsplayer is someone who follows by way of profession or life's work what is generally followed as a pastime or recreation by others.
A professional would list sport as the occupation he or she follows, or professes to be skilled in.

Until relatively recent times, to be a professional sportsplayer also said something about your status in society. It meant you were working class. Working-class sportsplayers, nearly always men, played for pay if they could. They were employees in a sports' industry but were always a small minority of all players.

Although the number of people earning a living from the sports industry has increased in recent years, the number of active professional sportsplayers remains quite small. In Britain today, for example, it has been estimated that there are 3,700 professional golfers, 3,700 professional tennis players, 2,000 professional footballers, 1,000 professional boxers and 200 professional jockeys.

- Television companies were prepared to pay large sums for the right to transmit pictures of the Games. However, becoming too dependent on one major source of funding could also threaten IOC control.
- The TOP programme meant a more diverse source of funds and therefore IOC independence. It enabled the IOC to claim that the Olympic Games was the only international sporting occasion where:
  - all the venues were free from advertisements
  - the athletes were not mobile advertisements
  - the executive officials of the various international sports organisations had total freedom to decide.

Sport: a proper business?

Professional sport has always been linked with business to some extent. The first professional matador in bullfighting in Spain, Francisco Romero, was born about 1700. Large sums could be earned in the bull ring even in the nineteenth century, and by the 1920s Juan Belmonte was receiving the equivalent of £2,500 for each *corrida* (bull fight). In Britain the jockey, Fred Archer, claimed an income of £8,000 in 1880. At that time, even ordinary jockeys could earn £1,000 a year when skilled workers would only have earned between £150 and £300. By 1900, boxers, athletes, cricketers and footballers formed a professional sporting elite, while the promoters of some sports events hoped to make profits too.

Sport, however, was not just another business. Its reorganisation by the educated middle classes in the late nineteenth century, was partly the result of their desire to ensure that sport was controlled by gentlemen. They felt that the paid player had to be kept in check. He could not be trusted to play fair if his livelihood was at stake and might therefore risk a foul in order to win. These middle-class reformers believed that sport was supposed to be for personal enjoyment, health and social improvement. It was not work, and it was not business either.

Yet, with some people prepared to pay to watch others play, sport *was* also a business. It was not like other businesses though. In sport, you need your rivals to stay in business so that they can provide the opposition for the next fight, match or race. You do not want to bankrupt them. So in football, for example, a maximum wage for professionals was introduced, dividends to shareholders were limited and directors went unpaid in order to ensure that football clubs survived. Profits were ploughed back, losses written off and success sought on the field.

The relationship between sport as business and sport as gentlemanly recreation was often a tense one. In the United States, business largely took over the national sport of baseball before the First World War, but in Britain the triumph of business was much longer delayed.

It was not until the 1960s that there was real evidence of change. Attendances had been falling at all sporting events for a decade. On the other hand, the paid player, especially in football, was demanding, and getting, an end to the old wage restrictions. The pressure was on to search for other sources of income. Television further complicated matters. By the 1970s some people, even in Britain, were beginning to talk about sport as an industry.

Amateur sportsplayer

An amateur is someone who is fond of or has a taste for something, and this could include sport. In the nineteenth century an amateur increasingly meant someone who cultivated sport as a pastime as against those professionals who pursued it as a livelihood.

To be called an amateur sportsplayer meant more than that, however. It was also a sign of higher social status – if you were an amateur you were also a lady or gentleman. Moreover, in Britain especially, it was bound up with a set of social rules about how life should be lived, as well as how sport should be played. This was summarised in the phrase 'fair play'.

British sporting relations with other countries were often disrupted by arguments about how to define an amateur player. The distinctions between amateur and professional have gradually been abandoned since the 1960s.

One reason why they were able to do this was because it was clear that people were spending more of their income on sport as part of their leisure. By the 1980s almost 2 per cent of total consumer spending in the Common Market was on sports goods and services. Even without gambling, it was greater than that spent on such things as electricity, furniture, do-it-yourself and video tapes.

Sports-related spending in Britain, 1986

Gambling	£1,600 million
Clothing and footwear	£770 million
Sports equipment	£690 million
Sports playing	£530 million
Total	£3,590 million

Sport was also a large employer of labour. By the mid 1980s it employed nearly 400,000 people in Britain alone. Such a figure was equivalent to the total number of workers employed in the chemical, man-made fibres, agriculture, forestry and fishing industries, and more than those employed in motor car manufacture and coal mining. In the European Community (EC) as a whole, the number of workers employed in the sports industry was as high as 2 million.

Sport was also good business for the government. In Britain it provided something like £2.4 billion in revenue by the mid 1980s:

VAT/excise duties	£770 million
Betting duty	£540 million
Income tax	£160 million

However, government spending on sport in Britain was only £545 million (although in 1987 local government spent a further £676 million on sport and physical recreation, in large part on its 850 sport centres, 130 golf courses and 2,500 swimming pools).

So even in Britain, where the idea of the gentleman amateur was so powerful for so long, sport is now big business. In 1987, Tottenham Hotspur plc's non-footballing business in clothes and sportswear accounted for over 30 per cent of their profits. At the beginning of the 1980s Aston Villa Football Club's commercial income was still only 7.5 per cent of their total revenue. By 1986/87, it had risen to 41 per cent. There is even a weekly paper now called *Sports Business*. If sport as business is flourishing, it is not surprising that the sports-goods industry is doing particularly well.

Looking the part

The manufacture of sports goods was once a small industry producing for a specialist market – equipment and clothing was aimed only at players. Bats, balls, boots, shoes, clubs, gloves, pads, racquets, shirts, shorts, skirts, socks and sticks were the mainstay. The growth of the sports industry has been good for sports retailing. Many sport and leisure centres now have their own sports shop which can provide up to 50 per cent of their total income.

What was a small, specialised industry has been turned into big business as sportswear has become mainstream fashion. Golf, skiing and tennis are known as the 'peacock sports' because, for many people, how you look is more important than how well you play. Many track suits are never worn close to a running track. A worldwide campaign of television advertising has helped to make trainers a status symbol for the young. The Nike advertisement exhorts the viewer to go out and get them – 'Just do it'. A recent study in London on mugging in Lambeth claimed that the main motive was the desire for expensive designer sportswear.

Only 20 per cent of sports shoes are bought for sport. Training shoes in particular have become a symbol of street style for many young people in Europe, America and Australia. The brand names – Reebok, Nike, Adidas, Puma – attract their own followers who often want the most up-to-date style, the most recent new design.

The sports goods company, Adidas, began its rise to power in the 1960s by offering free shoes and boots, equipment, and then cash, to athletes in a variety of sports, openly breaking the amateur rules in athletics and tennis. In 1976, Adidas claimed that 83 per cent of Olympic winners used its shoes and clothing. All Eastern European

Olympic athletes were equipped by Adidas. Adidas offered every national Olympic committee all the clothing and shoes they required for their competitors. The aim was to create a worldwide winning image which would persuade the ordinary person in the street to identify with their brand of leisure-wear. The company also sponsored certain key sportsmen, such as the Czech tennis player, Ivan Lendl. And as we saw on page 29, it was Adidas who brought the TOP idea to the International Olympic Committee.

Sponsorship

Sponsorship

The provision of funds or other forms of support for an event, for a commercial return.

Indeed, the most visible relationship between sport and business in the modern world is epitomised by the word sponsorship. Sports sponsorship has its own history. The popular British newspaper, *News of the World*, for example, sponsored match-play golf from 1903. It also met the costs of some inter-war athletics meetings, including those of the gentlemen-amateurs of Oxford and Cambridge Universities. The company Dunlop, as makers of golf equipment, began sponsoring tournaments from 1930. The Milk Marketing Board began sponsoring the round Britain cycle race – the Milk Race – in 1957. Other forms of commercial support were offered to local clubs, such as paying for the match ball, painting the company's name on the stand roof or advertising in the match programme. But it was all on a small scale until the 1970s. Even in 1971, only £2.5 million was spent on sports sponsorship in Britain; in 1990 it was thought to be in excess of £200 million. There are now over 100 organisations involved in the business of sports sponsorship.

Why do companies sponsor sport?
• To make the public more aware of them. The sponsoring company is provided with effective advertising by top-level sport because of the amount of time and space it gets in newspapers, in magazines, on radio and particularly on television. Almost 30 per cent of airtime on BBC 1 is devoted to sport, BBC 2 has around 34 per cent, ITV 21 per cent, and Channel 4 has 16 per cent. Sport is already a staple of cable and satellite channels. Moreover, sponsorship seems to work. Before Cornhill Insurance began sponsoring English Test Match cricket, for example, only 2 per cent of the population had heard of them: now 22 per cent have.

American tennis star, Jennifer Capriati: at the age of 15 she was already a millionaire and had sponsorship deals worth $6 million over 5 years.

33

- To sell more of their products. Companies like to promote particular brands rather than their corporate identity as a whole. The company Guinness, for example, promotes one product, Bell's whisky, at football matches, and another product, Pimms, at polo matches. This is rather than promoting the Guinness group as a whole.
- To provide corporate hospitality. Companies may sponsor sports events for a mixture of reasons which include entertaining clients or staff as well as promoting particular goods or services.

Cartoon from The Independent Magazine, 1990.

HENLEY ROYAL REGATTA

Henley Royal Regatta is the most relaxed, comfortable, authentic and treasured event in the British sporting and social calendar. It is a timeless occasion offering unrivalled style, sophistication and elegance, and all packaged in a fairytale setting.

Henley's five days of International competition and pure nostalgia bring a bustling carnival to the otherwise sleepy Oxfordshire town. A place to enjoy life to the full, and soak up the splendour of this truly Royal extravaganza. Henley Royal Regatta is more than an event – it is an unforgettable experience.

An aura of merriment, popping champagne corks and the scent of fresh strawberries and cream make Henley the epitome of an Edwardian English Summer.

Eights, Fours, Quadruple Sculls, Coxless Pairs and all manner of boating folk grace the waters of Henley Reach. The banks are alive with boaters and blazers, summer dresses and bonnets.

From Temple Island to Henley Bridge the world's finest oarsmen compete for some of Rowing's most treasured trophies. But not only is Henley Royal Regatta the Mecca of Rowing Men, it also provides unparalleled facilities for those in search of pleasure, atmosphere and the ultimate venue for summer entertaining. Henley is the place to be between June 29th and July 3rd.

For entertaining business colleagues or favoured friends a Keith Prowse Marquee with river frontage offers a unique environment in which to enjoy the magical charm of Henley's historic Royal Regatta. Your guests will be superbly cared for and catered for while you relax in comfort and luxury enjoying the splendour of one of England's most spectacular events.

Many businesses use corporate hospitality to entertain clients and sporting events are a popular choice.

Altruism and patronage can generally be ruled out in this strictly business relationship, but the National Westminster Bank's sponsorship activities make us pause for thought. Since 1977 they have been devoting 1 per cent of the pre-tax profits made by their high-street branches to sponsorship. However, they prefer to support community programmes rather than sport and when they do support it, youth or minority sports are chosen. In 1988 their programme director explained:

We wanted to help keep the community on an even keel – riots and the like are no good to us, no good for business confidence, no good to anybody.

Companies usually look carefully before deciding about sponsorship, and the reasons for their choices are sometimes complex. Why should Barclays Bank have decided to sponsor League Football in England in the 1980s? Heysel, Hillsborough and hooliganism gave it an ugly image. On the positive side, though, football was still the most popular sport and all ages were interested in it. There were over 2,000 matches in a season lasting from August to May. Television showed some of those games to about 40 different countries and Barclays could offer hospitality to its clients in most of the major towns in England and Wales. But the key to Barclay's decision was probably the fact that the bank wanted to foster a younger image. The coincidence that the chairman is a Tottenham Hotspur supporter had *nothing* to do with it!

Finally, why did a Norwegian fertiliser firm sponsor the National Village Cricket knock-out championship in Britain? A total number of 630 clubs and 7,000 players are eventually reduced to 2 clubs and 22 players on a late August day at Lords. What was in it for Norsk Hydro?

It is probably safe to say that without sponsorship a good deal of organised sport would find it difficult to survive in its present form. This is especially true of cricket, football and rugby (league and union), and all motor sports. In 1988, 3,000 manufacturing companies were involved in football sponsorship alone. Where survival is at stake, temptation can be great. Some critics allege that sport has come to rely too heavily on sponsorship by the makers of alcohol and tobacco.

Who spends what where

The big spenders: the top twelve sponsorship deals in Britain, August–October 1989

Rank	Sponsor	Amount/deal's timespan	Event or sponsored body
1	Barclays	£7m/three years	Football League
2	Scottish Brewers	£2.5m/three years	Scottish Rugby Union League (extension)
3	Tennent's	£2.5m/four years	Scottish Cup (football)
4	Alloa Brewers (SKOL)	£1m	Scottish Skol Cup (football)
5	British Gas	£750,000/three years	Bobby Charlton's sports schools
6	British Coal	£750,000/four years	Great Britain rugby league squad
7	B&Q	£612,000	Scottish Premier football league, first and second divisions
8	Commercial Union	£410,000/three years	Universities Athletic Union
9	Hanson Trust	£300,000	British Sports Trust
10	General Accident	£250,000	Golf 'skins' game for charity
11	GrandMet	£250,000/three years	National Association of Boys' Clubs
12	Whitbread (Heineken)	£250,000/three years	Hockey's club league championship event

Source: Marketing, November 1989

Smoking out a winner

Spontaneous awareness of sponsorship deals, June–August 1989. How successful have companies been in promoting their products through sport? Are they getting value for money from their sponsorship? How many sports are associated with smoking and drinking?

Rank	Sponsor	Sport	% rating
1	Embassy	Snooker	34
2	Mars	Marathon	32
3	Barclays	Football	24
4	Benson and Hedges	Snooker	20
5=	Benson and Hedges	Cricket	19
5=	Milk	Cycling	19
7=	Embassy	Darts	14
7=	Marlboro	Motorsport	14
9	Cornhill	Cricket	13
10=	Littlewoods	Football	13
10=	John Player	Motorsport	12
12=	Shell	Motorsport	11
12=	Rothmans	Snooker	11

Source: Marketing, November 1989

35

Sport is still attractive because of its vigorous, healthy, wholesome, youthful image. But in 1987, 20 per cent of sports sponsorship in Britain was paid for by the makers of cigarettes and alcohol. In the same year there were over 100,000 premature deaths from smoking, and more than 40,000 from alcohol-related illness. Drink was a factor in many other social problems too. Swimming refused sponsorship from these sources, but cricket, football, motor sport, rugby, snooker and darts have all accepted sponsorship money from alcohol and tobacco companies.

Since 1985 tobacco companies have not been allowed to advertise on television, but by sponsoring sporting events which they know will be televised they gain a large amount of advertising. Out of the top twenty sports on television, seven are sponsored by the tobacco trade. The companies claim that they are merely encouraging people who smoke already to change to another brand, but can we believe that the aim is not to recruit new smokers too?

If sport is now a business, and largely kept going not by revenue from participants or spectators, but by the support of other businesses, does it matter? Here are some reasons why it might.

- Business and sport are not the same. Business always needs to win. The notion of winning at any price can only undermine the values of sport.
- How do the values of sport differ from those of business? Both are competitive. Both reward success. But sport is also for promoting enjoyment, participation, fair play and a fair chance. Can those values survive a business take-over?
- Business has an inner compulsion to expand. The Olympics is one example, and the World Cup perhaps another, of a good sporting event becoming monstrous in size under commercial pressures to have more sports and/or more competitors.
- Business sponsorship puts pressure on athletes to run and players to play even when it is against their own interests to do so. Too much sport poses a physical threat to the performers. Is it even in the interest of the paying customer for competitors to be compelled to play when they ought to be resting?
- Sport has been a kind of democracy based on voluntary principles and the efforts of many unpaid workers, especially in Britain. But will those companies who pay the money increasingly want to call the tune – change the rules, alter the course, arrange the schedules – to suit themselves? Will it matter if football becomes a game of four quarters instead of two halves? Can sport maintain its integrity and autonomy if someone else is paying the bills?

With unambiguous evidence that drinking and smoking damage physical and social health, should the manufacturers of those products be allowed to sponsor sport?

4 Watching sport

The view from the terrace

Sport has always attracted a crowd. Indeed some critics would argue that the crowd is a crucial part of the experience. Crowds add to the excitement and uncertainty. The presence of spectators may influence the players, affect their concentration, frighten them or urge them on to greater efforts.

Sporting crowds are not neutral. A former manager of Liverpool Football Club, Bill Shankly, claimed that the Liverpool supporters were the only professional spectators in the game: 'They have made an art of supporting a team and by doing so, have played a big part in the success of Liverpool.' Certainly many people who believe that watching sport is not a passive but an active experience feel that the crowd contributes to an atmosphere which can influence the outcome.

Why do people pay to watch others play? Opportunities for experiencing strong excitement are rare in the modern world. At sporting events, however, fans can do things – shout, wave their arms, jump up and down, swear at the referee – which would be frowned upon elsewhere. Spectator sports are social occasions which give people a chance to belong to a larger group and to support the team or individual representing that group. Being part of the crowd on such occasions might reinforce political or religious beliefs. It can often be an emotionally draining experience, but it's an experience which can be shared with friends.

It is clear that some sports have always been more attractive to spectators than others. Football is a truly whole-world game: there is hardly a country where it does not draw big crowds. Rugby is the national sport in New Zealand and South Africa. In the United States, the largely home-grown sports of baseball, basketball and American football are the most popular. Cycling is a crowd-puller in Western Europe, especially France. Top motor sport and speedway attracts enthusiasts in many rich countries. In China, table tennis has been remarkably popular, while in Japan baseball and sumo wrestling always draw big crowds. Golf and tennis have increased the size of their following in the world's richest countries. However, few people would pay to watch swimming or squash, hockey or gymnastics. Once a sport becomes established in a country – a process which took place in many parts of the world between about 1880 and 1920 – it usually remains popular there in spite of competition from sports from elsewhere. History, and what comes to be called tradition, are powerful supports for sport.

Which sport you watch usually depends on what you were brought up with. If you are introduced to a sport at an early age, when powerful loyalties are often made, it can last a lifetime. Like jobs, sport was often passed on from fathers to sons – more rarely from mothers to daughters or fathers to daughters. For many youngsters, in many different cultures, sport remains an important strand in their relationship with their parents.

Fanzines are magazines written by and for football fans. Some fanzines deal with soccer in general, others with a particular club. Hard-hitting fanzines such as 'When Saturday Comes' and 'Off the ball' give editors and readers the chance to criticise the football authorities and media coverage, and to reflect the views of genuine supporters.

The reasons for watching sport have probably not changed much over time, but the context certainly has. In the 1930s, for example, a trip to, say, a football match in Britain or a baseball game in the United States would have probably meant travelling to the ground on foot or by public transport and paying for entry at the gate to the stadium. The price of entry would have been cheap. The crowd would have been male and not particularly young. Every sport had its season: football was a winter game, baseball a summer one. Many spectators felt that it was a privilege to be there because only those actually present could feel the tension and see the play. Other interested parties would have to read about it in the papers after the event, or perhaps listen to part of it described by a radio commentator.

In the 1990s the business of going to a game is very different. Travel to the ground is quite likely to be by private car. The crowd will have more women members and will probably be younger. Many spectators will be season ticket holders. In the 1930s most people stood to watch British football matches; by the end of the 1990s most will sit. The cost of watching is no longer cheap. Advancing technology has meant that others can watch in the comfort of their homes at the same time as the spectator in the stadium. And everywhere, the police presence at matches has been greatly expanded.

Crowd violence

Crowds at sporting events, especially football matches, are often large. Being part of such a crowd can be exhilarating but also dangerous. People can panic, especially if too many are confined in a small space and crowds can sometimes get out of control. Most of the world's worst sporting tragedies were accidents caused when crowds at football matches behaved unpredictably or responded in panic to some external pressure.

The following incident, which took place in the Lenin Stadium in Moscow, in 1982, shows how quickly such behaviour can lead to catastrophe. Three hundred and forty people died, crushed on a stairway, when a last-minute goal by Moscow Spartak against Haarlem of Holland brought departing spectators rushing back into the ground. It was remarkably similar to the disaster at Ibrox Park, Glasgow, in 1971, when 66 people were trampled or suffocated to death on a stairway, following a last-minute goal in the game between Rangers and Celtic. The deaths at Hillsborough in 1989 will long remain fresh in the memory of many people in Britain. It is clear the disaster was caused by overcrowding at one end of the ground.

All these were tragic accidents. The events at the Heysel Stadium in Brussels, in 1985, seemed even worse because of how they occurred. In this incident 39 spectators, 31 of them Italian supporters of Juventus, were crushed or trampled to death when trying to escape a charge by Liverpool supporters. This event led to English football clubs being banned from European competition for five years. It was the most serious manifestation to date of what had come to be labelled 'football hooliganism'.

Hooligan

The word 'hooligan' is slang for a rough, lawless young person. The phrase 'football hooligan' entered the English language in the 1970s.

Football hooligans

A small minority of young males appear to use watching sport in general, but football in particular, as an opportunity to fight with similar groups of supporters of the opposing side. Football hooliganism has often been called the English disease but England has no monopoly on this sort of violence. Fighting among groups of football supporters takes place to some extent in most of the countries of Europe and is by no means unknown elsewhere from Africa to China and Egypt to Latin America.

It is not only football which provides the occasion for fighting fans. One survey from the United States, for example, listed 312 sports-related riots in 12 years between 1960 and 1972. Many of them took place in high schools where traditional local rivalries were aggravated by ethnic and racial differences. However, violence linked to football has received the most attention and the heaviest criticism in the media, and is probably the worst case.

A victim of violence at the football ground: a Manchester United fan with a dart stuck in his face.

Who are the so-called 'football hooligans'? Why do they rampage, and can anything be done to stop it? It used to be thought that the typical offender was young, male and unskilled or unemployed. It still appears to be the case that most of those involved are males between the ages of 14 and 30, but recent research has suggested that more football hooligans have skilled or clerical jobs than was once thought. When offenders are asked why they do it, they often mention the excitement and claim that fighting at football matches is an assertion of maleness.

Research suggests that as policing at grounds has grown stricter, football hooligans have got better organised and more vicious. One estimate claims that their activities cause about six deaths a year.

What can be done? Football clubs have been encouraged to involve themselves more in the activities of their communities. Various educational efforts aimed at pointing out the dangers of hooliganism and attempting to teach fair play have begun in schools. Strict policing and segregation inside grounds appear to have contained violence although certainly not eradicated it. Other suggestions have included involving ordinary supporters in the running and organisation of clubs, and trying to attract more women to matches. Sensational reporting in newspapers has also been criticised.

Perhaps the issue needs to be placed in the wider context of anti-social behaviour by young males in places other than football grounds. The 14–20-year-old male age group contains the highest number of offenders cautioned or found guilty in the courts. We have already noted how sport is closely linked to emotion. Perhaps it is not surprising, especially in a group of this age range, that their emotion sometimes spills over. Working to limit the number of occasions when that happens is, however, a difficult task.

Cleaning up: trying to influence behaviour at Northampton Town Football Club.

Televised sport

In most industrial countries, fewer people watch others playing sport now than did so in the 1940s and 1950s. For the ones who do, top sport has become more expensive and therefore more exclusive.

In Britain, this is only partly due to the aftermath of Lord Justice Taylor's report on the Hillsborough disaster, which recommended expensive improvements to grounds. Seats have been replacing standing places, and businesses have been renting boxes for the privileged few, which also means less room for ordinary followers. For example, the ten big companies who sponsored the Olympic Games had over 10,000 of their guests present at the Seoul Olympics in 1988. However, if you cannot get into a top sporting event you can always watch it on television. That may not be true for much longer, but at present it is on television that most people increasingly watch their sport.

Sport 'on the box'

The rush hour started early .... By 7 pm the pubs were packed, city centres were deserted, and the curtains were drawn in the nation's sitting rooms. It was the night of the World Cup semi-final between England and West Germany, and Britain had become a television village.

With 21.5 million homes in Britain with TV sets, the potential audience for any programme is 52.8 million. On the summer evening of 4 July, the number of viewers ... was 25,210,000. It was the biggest audience for any single event in British television history, achieved in a period when television viewing is declining.

The Guardian, 13 August 1990

This massive audience was divided equally between men and women. Sport on television rarely does that well but, unlike most television programmes, sport is usually live and always unpredictable. It also attracts enough viewers to appeal to TV companies and advertisers alike. Television has become one of the major influences working to reshape world sport.

Showing sport on British television has always been seen as a social duty. In 1954 the Postmaster-General, a Government Minister, declared six sporting occasions to be national events. This meant they belonged to everyone and neither the BBC nor the new channel, ITV, were to have exclusive rights to them. The Cup Final, the Boat Race, the Derby and the Grand National, Test Match cricket and Wimbledon were key dates on the national sporting calendar. In the event there was not much competition between ITV and BBC at first. Sport did not seem such an audience-puller and the BBC had built up a good relationship with the governing bodies of those sports it valued.

Technological change did much to make sport on television more attractive. Video recording, editing of the action, slow-motion replays, communication satellites which enabled live transmission around the world, and especially colour – without which snooker would never have appealed to the armchair audience – changed the nature of television sport. By the 1970s, ITV was much more interested in competing for sport, and especially those sports that advertisers were keen on. By the mid 1980s, ITV had bought exclusive rights to gymnastics, athletics and league football.

None of these changes threatened the position of the viewer but the rise of satellite television does. German viewers, for example, were unable to watch their tennis players, Boris Becker and Steffi Graf, win the Wimbledon singles championships in 1989, because the television rights had been sold to a satellite channel to which most households had no access. In Britain, the Broadcasting Act of 1990 means that all rights to broadcast sport can be sold to the highest bidder after existing contracts run out. Opinion polls showed 75 per cent of those asked opposed the change. An early result was that few could watch the 1992 Cricket World Cup Final because the rights had been bought by a satellite company. The same thing has happened with live Premier League football.

Sports most enjoyed on television in Britain

	1969		1989	
	%	Ranking	%	Ranking
Snooker	17	20th	43	1st
Athletics	45	3rd	37	2nd
Tennis	38	8th	30	3rd
Soccer	52	1st	29	4th
Boxing	43	7th	27	5th
Skating	44	4th	25	6th
Darts	–	–	24	7th
Cricket	31	12th	23	8th
Motor racing	32	11th	23	9th
Golf	23	16th	23	10th
Skiing	35	9th	22	11th
Bowls	–	–	20	12th
Showjumping	49	2nd	19	13th
Rugby union	21	17th	18	14th
Wrestling	44	5th	17	15th
Swimming	43	6th	15	16th
American football	–	–	15	17th
Motor cycling	29	13th	15	18th
Rugby league	25	15th	14	19th
Horse racing	33	10th	13	20th

Source: S. Barnett, *Games and Sets: the changing faces of sport on television,* 1990

Viewing in the USA

A comparison with the United States is interesting. They have no equivalent to the BBC but they do have three enormous national corporations – ABC, CBS and NBC. In 1956, CBS paid the American football governing body $1 million for the television rights for that season. By 1982, the growth of the audience and the interest of advertisers prompted the big three networks to pay the National Football League (NFL) $26 billion for a five-year contract. Such a staggering sum meant that each team in the NFL received $15 million every year before playing a match or selling a ticket.

Perhaps major British sports will be able to sell their product to BBC, ITV and the satellite companies jointly. However, the popularity of sport on television in the United States seems greater than in Britain. When the broadcasting of a live NFL match changed to Monday nights it led to Tuesday replacing Monday as the peak of absenteeism in the car factories of Detroit!

Massive amounts of money can be made by both the television companies and the sports themselves. In 1984, ABC paid $2.25 million to show the Los Angeles Olympics. They found sponsors willing to pay as much as $520,000 a minute to advertise during transmissions from the Games, and ABC made a profit of $650 million.

Too high a price?

However, there is another price to be paid in television's willingness to intervene directly in the internal affairs of sport.

- Television insists on deciding when events will start and how long they will last in order to suit their schedules. At the 1989 Adelaide motor racing Grand Prix, for example, heavy rain forced a delay of half an hour. Drivers were then bullied back onto a soaked track because expensive satellite time had been booked for a limited period. In 1970 and 1986 in Mexico, World Cup football matches were played in the midday heat to suit television.

- Television will try to change the rules of sport to bring more concentrated excitement. In Britain, recent examples have been shorter matches in snooker and bowls, and one-day cricket. The tie-break in tennis was TV-inspired too. In America, the North American Soccer League was told that if it wanted television coverage, then goal-less draws were out. It had to agree to a fifteen-minute period of first-to-score-wins extra time, followed by a shoot-out.
- In 1994 the World Cup will be held in the United States. American television craves action and in soccer that means goals. The 1990 World Cup in Italy produced the lowest-ever goals-per-game average since the competition began in 1930. American television has been putting the world governing body, FIFA, under pressure to increase the width of the goal-mouth in time for 1994.
- Coverage can be distorted. During the first days of the Seoul Olympics in 1988, NBC learned that fewer Americans were watching than advertisers had been promised. Clients had to be compensated by being given amounts of free air time. This meant more advertising breaks at the expense of the sport.
- Television money has led to huge salaries for the players, especially in America. This may encourage a win-at-all-costs attitude. It may also, as happens more widely in athletics, put pressure on the stars to appear on the track more often than is physically or mentally good for them.
- In general, there is a danger that money from television will benefit the few top players, their agents, and a small number of big sports promoters, far more than it will benefit the rest of the sport.

Television sport is an ideal international product. It is relatively cheap to produce, it is popular and it leaps the language barrier. This is especially true of big events like the Olympics and the World Cup. Television allows even English soccer to reach a world audience in 48 different countries via a weekly highlights programme. This audience, from Denmark to Australia, Uganda to China, is estimated to be in excess of 50 million. This brings us back to where we began: the World Cup match between England and West Germany, which was a national occasion, linking most people in the nation. Will this be possible in an age of multi-channel competition?

Some argue that television has saved sport from economic collapse. As costs have soared and fewer people have been prepared to pay at the gate, television has provided much-needed revenue from both right-to-show payments and sponsorship. Others say that the price has not been right and that top sport is being corrupted by money. It is becoming too competitive, and is not even a branch of the entertainments industry any more but a branch of the advertising industry. It is being reshaped for the television audience at the expense of the paying punter.

The enthusiast would probably agree with the Russian composer, Dmitri Shostakovich, a football fan: 'How can television soccer compare with the fantastic impact of watching a match at the stadium? It's like distilled water and export Stolichnaya!'

5 Sport and politics

The Olympic Games

International sporting contest held every four years since its modern revival in 1896. The Olympic Games was originally a great festival held every fourth year in honour of the God Zeus at Olympia, a plain in ancient Greece.

In late nineteenth-century Britain, most affluent people who were interested in sport saw it as separate from other areas of their lives: separate from work, separate from religion and certainly separate from politics. A minority of influential Britons, aided by foreign sympathisers, tried to persuade the world that sport was play and nothing but.

The attempt failed. Sport takes place in society and people will make of it what they will. Some will make it their business, some will use it to sustain religious belief and some will try to exploit its political potential. To maintain, as many people within sport the world over do, that politics should be kept out of sport, is itself a political statement.

We have been looking at the nature of sport – but what about politics? Politics is about the way governments make policy and the different views political parties have about what that policy should be. Where there are differences of opinion about what decisions should be taken there will be politics. International sport in particular, bringing, as it must, competition between individuals and teams from different nations, is always likely to reflect the political conflicts of the time. The Olympic Games has always been a political as well as a sporting event.

BRITAIN'S STRENGTH
IS THE TEAM SPIRIT
National Labour
IS PLAYING ITS PART
IN THE
NATIONAL GOVERNMENT
TEAM

National Labour's political pamplet. Even in the 1930s, politicians wanted to associate with successful sportsmen.

The Olympic Games

The International Olympic Committee was formed in 1894 and the first modern Games was held in Athens in 1896. Although the original aim of the Games was to provide an opportunity for athletes from different countries to compete with one another, practical problems of organisation meant that nation-states would be the basic units. That in turn meant that the politics of international prestige were soon involved. It was decided very early on that only those athletes wearing state colours could take part and that athletes should parade at the beginning of the Games behind national flags.

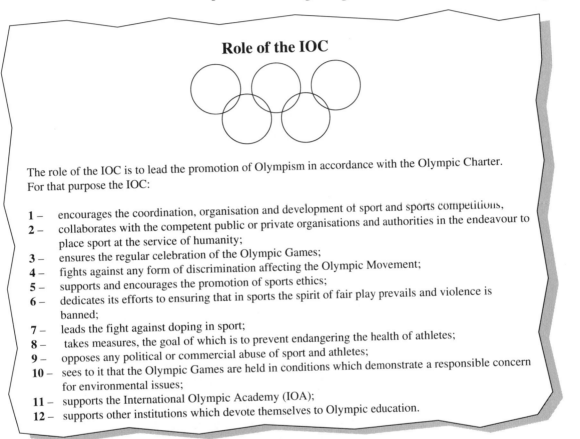

Role of the IOC

The role of the IOC is to lead the promotion of Olympism in accordance with the Olympic Charter.
For that purpose the IOC:

1 – encourages the coordination, organisation and development of sport and sports competitions,
2 – collaborates with the competent public or private organisations and authorities in the endeavour to place sport at the service of humanity;
3 – ensures the regular celebration of the Olympic Games;
4 – fights against any form of discrimination affecting the Olympic Movement;
5 – supports and encourages the promotion of sports ethics;
6 – dedicates its efforts to ensuring that in sports the spirit of fair play prevails and violence is banned;
7 – leads the fight against doping in sport;
8 – takes measures, the goal of which is to prevent endangering the health of athletes;
9 – opposes any political or commercial abuse of sport and athletes;
10 – sees to it that the Olympic Games are held in conditions which demonstrate a responsible concern for environmental issues;
11 – supports the International Olympic Academy (IOA);
12 – supports other institutions which devote themselves to Olympic education.

Uniform dress was worn. Medal ceremonies also involved national flags and anthems. This produced conflicts like those in 1912, when Austria-Hungary refused to allow the Czechs to enter a separate team. There was no Czechoslovakia at that time – the Czech people lived in Bohemia, which was not an independent country, but part of the Austro-Hungarian Empire. Similarly, the Finns were compelled to march behind the Russian flag because they lived under Russian rule. As recently as 1976, James Gilkes of Guyana tried to compete as an individual when his national Olympic association withdrew from the Games, but he was refused permission by the International Olympic Committee.

The choice of site for the Games has been political too. Antwerp was selected in 1920 to emphasise the recovery of Belgium from the attack by Germany in 1914. The Germans in turn were punished for causing the First World War by not being allowed to compete in

1920 and 1924. However, when the decision was taken in 1930, to hold the Games of 1936 in Germany, this clearly signalled Germany's return to equal status in the community of nations. Unfortunately, before these Games were held, Hitler and the Nazis came to power (in 1933). The Nazis immediately took over control of all sport and proclaimed it to be as political as everything else:

> *'German athletes are in the complete sense of the word, political. It is impossible for individuals or private clubs to indulge in physical exercise and games. These are the business of the state.'*

> *Daily Telegraph*, January 4 1936

Jesse Owens at the Berlin Olympics, 1936.

The International Olympic Committee (IOC) did not agree with this but chose to ignore it. Others tried to organise a boycott of the 1936 Berlin Games as a protest against Germany's treatment of Jews, trade unionists and other radicals, many of whom had been placed in concentration camps. But the boycott failed. Most athletes just wanted to compete and refused to see that Germany would not allow everyone the chance to do so.

When the Olympics was resumed after the Second World War, in 1948, London was chosen as the venue, partly as a reward for Britain's part in the Allied war effort and partly as a sign that Britain was on the road to recovery. Tokyo's selection in 1960 also indicated that Japan was back among the community of nations, following her wartime alliance with Nazi Germany.

By that time, the Cold War (see page 49) between West and East, between the United States and the Soviet Union, was in full swing. This was inevitably reflected in the Olympics. The Soviet Union first sent a team to the Games in 1952 – it had not competed in the Olympics since the Revolution of 1917. It was soon clear that both the Soviet Union and the United States were prepared to use their performance in the Games as a sign of the strength of their respective social systems. Both took advantage of an Olympic Charter which declared the games non-political but allowed the idea of a medal table.

Moreover, there was a political wrangle over who should represent Germany. The Americans and their allies in the West refused to recognise the Russian zone of Germany as a separate independent state – the German Democratic Republic (East Germany). Between 1952 and 1964 the two Germanies – East and West – competed under a compromise flag and a compromise anthem. The DDR (Deutsche Demokratische Republik, or East Germany) wanted recognition of their independence. Some international sports organisations eventually did this, the IOC included, so that two German teams competed separately in Mexico in 1968. When the East Germans marched behind their own flag and had their own anthem at the Munich Games of 1972, it symbolised the practical recognition of the East German state by the West.

The Mexico City Games of 1968 were politically significant in two respects. Mexico was the first developing nation to stage them. It was an attempt by Mexico to show it had the power and the resources of the major industrial nations. But it was used by the Opposition to stage pre-Olympic demonstrations which were savagely put down by the army, with much loss of life. It was also in the Olympics of 1968, before millions of television viewers throughout the world, that the two black American sprinters, Tommy Smith and John Carlos, who had just finished first and third in the 200 metres, gave the black power salute at the victory ceremony in protest against racism in the United States. Tommy Smith declared:

'If I win I am an American, not a Black American. But if I did something bad then they would say "a Negro". We are black and we are proud of being black.'

Sprinters Tommy Smith and John Carlos on the rostrum at the 1968 Olympics. As they were presented with their medals and the US anthem was played, they made a gesture for black power, and fair treatment of black American athletes. Were they wrong to 'use' the Olympics in this way? Or were they acting within the principles of the Olympics by exposing a social injustice which affects sport?

Boycott

To refuse to have any dealings with a person, organisation or country, as a means of protest, or to force change. The word comes from the case of Captain Boycott, land agent in Ireland in the nineteenth century, who was a victim of such a practice for refusing to reduce rents.

Boycotting sport

In 1972, the Munich Games were used by Arab terrorists to kill a group of Israeli athletes and promote their cause. The Games continued, however, with the IOC claiming it would be a victory for political extremism if they did not.

By 1972 there had already been other examples of countries boycotting the Olympics for political purposes. Sports boycotts were and are very appealing. They cost the boycotting government no money. They hurt few people directly and they can be interpreted as a sporting matter rather than a direct attack on another country. For example, Holland, Spain and Switzerland refused to go to the Melbourne Games in 1956 as a protest at the recent invasion of Hungary by Soviet troops. Egypt, Lebanon and Iraq stayed away as a sign of displeasure with the combined British–French–Israeli occupation of the Suez Canal in 1956.

A much more widespread refusal to take part in the Montreal Games of 1976 was aimed at the apartheid policies of South Africa (see page 51). Thirty states boycotted the Games because New Zealand had sent a team. New Zealand had earlier played a series of rugby tests against South Africa, who had already been expelled from the Olympic movement.

The United States opposed this boycott on the grounds that politics should be kept out of sport. But in 1980, with the Games due to be held in Moscow, the Americans withdrew in protest at the Soviet invasion of Afghanistan the year before. The American Government put a lot of pressure on the US Olympic Committee: 'national security' was said to be at stake and the Committee eventually voted 2 to 1 not to go. Canada did the same.

The British Government fully supported the American boycott and called on the British Olympic Association (BOA) to join in. There were full-day debates in the House of Commons and the House of Lords. Both produced resolutions calling for British withdrawal from the Games. Never had a sporting matter received such parliamentary attention. The Prime Minister, Mrs Thatcher, wrote three times to the BOA asking them to withdraw: she even offered £50 million of taxpayers' money to help resite the games. But all the pressure failed. The BOA said it was up to the governing bodies of each individual sport to decide whether to compete or not. With a few exceptions, all chose to go to Moscow, where Britain had the fourth largest team. The Sports Council, which is funded by the government and whose chairman is appointed by the Department of the Environment, refused to support the boycott.

What this episode demonstrated was that in a country like Britain, where the Government has played little part in the running of sport, and there is a strong tradition of civil freedom, sport can resist political pressure. The Government failed to unify the country behind the boycott. A sum of £800,000 was raised to support those athletes who wished to go.

It was ironic that many of those people who normally attached themselves to the slogan 'Keep politics out of sport' were most active in the boycott campaign.

The Cold War

The American boycott of the Olympics in Moscow in 1980, and the 'tit for tat' Russian retaliation in Los Angeles in 1984, now appear as almost the final sporting gestures of the Cold War. Both the major

Cold War

A state of political hostility, but involving no actual fighting. In the late 1940s, after the Second World War, a period of Cold War began between the Western bloc countries (Western Europe, Canada and the USA) and the Eastern bloc countries (Eastern Europe and the USSR). It came to an end in 1989, as Communist regimes collapsed across Eastern Europe.

powers had realised quite early that sport could be used as a weapon in the battle between two opposing political systems and ways of life. When the Russians entered the Olympics in 1952 they brought with them a scoring system which placed more emphasis on strength in depth than in simply winning numerous gold medals. Each side had its own way of calculating victory at the Olympics and both could claim to have won.

But sport could also be used to indicate a wish to become more friendly as well as a method of showing disapproval. For example, London entertained a team from Moscow in an athletics match in 1954 and this was the first of a series of meetings which commentators interpreted as a sign of improved East–West relations. The matches were only temporarily interrupted in 1956 when the British Government said it could not get a law court to drop charges against a female Russian shot-putter accused of stealing three hats from a London shop.

These contacts between East and West signalled a new Russian attitude following the death of Stalin in 1953, and the criticism of his ruthless regime at the Twentieth Communist Party Congress in 1956. They were part of Nikita Khruschev's policy of 'peaceful co-existence'. This meant that the two systems – capitalism and communism – were still in competition, but by all means short of war.

In 1958 the two 'superpowers' signed the first in a series of agreements on cultural, educational and technical exchanges. The first athletics match between the USA and the USSR took place the same year. These sporting contacts helped prepare the ground for Mr Khruschev's famous visit to America in 1959. However, the athletics match between the two countries was cancelled in 1966 as part of Russian disapproval of American involvement in the Vietnam War, and in particular its bombing of North Vietnam.

Sporting contacts do not solve political problems but in the context of the Cold War they probably did something to reduce each side's fear of the other. On the other hand, they also provided a continuing reminder of 'superpower' rivalry.

Sport was also used on a famous occasion to signify the re-entry of Communist China into world politics, when an American table-tennis team visited the country in 1971. In a blaze of publicity, the visit apparently led to a rapid shift in the way the American people thought about 'Red China'. Because it was a meeting for sport, however, it did not mean that any definite political commitment had been made on either side.

Of course it is the context – the circumstances – which provide political meaning to a sports event. In 1968, the Soviet Army invaded Czechoslovakia because it did not approve of the Government's reforms there. The next year the two nations met in the world ice-hockey championships. The Czechs won, provoking riotous anti-Russian celebrations both in the streets of Prague and even in the state-controlled newspapers. So sport was a well-nigh perfect weapon for the Cold War, and sporting contacts – or the lack of them – was a sign of whether Russian–American relations were warm or frosty.

South Africa

Perhaps the most famous international example of the relationship between sport and politics in the modern world has been the case of South Africa. In that country a minority of 4 million whites has dominated a majority of 20 million black, Asian and coloured peoples by a deliberate Government policy of separate and unequal development. South Africa was a racially segregated country. The State decided where you lived, where and how you were educated, and even limited your choice of marriage partner. It also controlled who you could play sport with and where you could watch it. Sporting facilities for whites were much better than those for non-whites. By the mid 1950s, racially integrated sport had been banned by the Government.

When a black weight-lifter called Precious Mackenzie surmounted all the obstacles to beat all the white competitors in his class, he was still not chosen for the South African team to go to the 1960 Olympics. The team that went to Rome was all white. It was to be the last for 32 years.

The 1960s saw a series of changes in the world which were to lead to South Africa's political and sporting isolation.

- The decade saw a hardening of racial attitudes among white South Africans.
- It saw a liberalising of attitudes elsewhere, especially in Europe and America.
- It saw a large group of African countries claiming their independence from their former European rulers. Many countries

Apartheid

This is a system invented by the white Government of South Africa in 1948. In the language of Afrikaans, *apartheid* means 'apart-ness'. Its purpose was to keep black and white people apart.

The system of apartheid, under which the black African majority of 20 million was dominated by the white minority of 4 million and denied basic freedoms and the benefits of the country's great wealth, was enshrined in South Africa's laws. International pressure has forced some change in South Africa in recent years. Many laws of apartheid have now been dismantled, although critics argue that there is still a long way to go.

such as Kenya, Uganda and Tanzania joined the British Commonwealth, which South Africa left in 1961.
• The continuing Cold War provided Africans with a supporter against South Africa: the USSR.

In 1962, the South African Government announced that no racially mixed teams should take part in sport either inside or outside South Africa. Three years later, in 1965, the President of South Africa reaffirmed that black Maori rugby players in New Zealand touring sides would not be allowed in South Africa.

In 1968, pressure from African and Asian nations resulted in a Commission from the International Olympic Committee visiting South Africa to investigate black sporting opportunities. The Commission said that non-white athletes had adequate facilities and coaching. They were pleased that the South African Olympic Committee had agreed to send a multi-racial team to the 1968 Olympic Games. The Commission recommended that South Africa should be welcomed back into the Olympic movement.

Black Africa was outraged. The Organisation for African Unity called for a boycott, which all 32 African nations threatened to join. Islamic and Caribbean nations pledged support. Some black American athletes signed a petition to the American Olympic Committee urging that South Africa should not be allowed to enter the Games. The result of this pressure was that the IOC's invitation to South Africa was withdrawn.

By 1970, therefore, South Africa was banned from taking part in most international sport and the campaign against apartheid in sport was growing. A planned cricket tour of Britain scheduled for that year was called off, partly because it would have been difficult to play the matches in the face of organised political opposition. The rugby tour of Britain in 1969 had only survived due to the large-scale policing of the matches. In May 1970, the IOC meeting in Amsterdam voted 35–28 to expel South Africa from the Olympic movement.

Only a few countries retained any sporting links with South Africa and pressure was growing on them to give them up. New Zealand was the most important of these. Rugby was the national game in both countries. The New Zealand Rugby Union toured South Africa in 1970 – and included three Maoris and one Samoan for the first time – and they returned in 1976. Thirty African nations withdrew from the Montreal Olympics of 1976 in protest. The threat of a similar boycott of the 1978 Commonwealth Games in Edmonton prompted delegates at the Commonwealth Conference at Gleneagles in 1977 to agree to 'discourage contact or competition by their nationals with sporting organisations, teams, or sportsmen from South Africa or from any other country where sports are organised on the basis of race, colour or ethnic origin'. This did not prevent New Zealand welcoming rugby tourists from South Africa in 1981, including the first coloured member of the team, Errol Tobias. It led directly to fifteen African countries boycotting the 1982 Commonwealth Games.

By this time the United Nations was producing a register of all those who had sporting contacts with South Africa. It was a kind of blacklist. Another sign of the changing times came in 1985 when the proposed New Zealand rugby tour was called off. The High Court in New Zealand declared that because of the political situation in South Africa, such a tour would be contrary to the constitutional aims of the New Zealand Rugby Union, which were to promote and foster the game. That could not be done in South African conditions.

The response in South Africa has taken three main forms.

- Some individuals and organisations have tried to foster sport among the different ethnic groups and move towards integration.
- Some leading sportsmen and women, barred from international sport, have left the republic and tried to qualify for other countries. The most notorious case was that of Zola Budd. In 1984 Britain waived immigration restrictions so that she could qualify for the British Olympic team on the grounds that she had a British grandfather. She is now married and resettled in South Africa.
- Some South African companies attempted to undermine the policy of isolation by offering large sums of money to professional sports players and administrators to play in South Africa. South African breweries were alleged to have spent £1.2 million on the 1982 tour by English cricketers which led to several of them being banned from international cricket, including Graham Gooch, who was banned for three years. In 1983 a black West Indian team were allegedly paid $100,000 per man to tour. They received life bans in Jamaica and Guyana.

How effective are sporting boycotts in bringing about change? Refusing to play sport with South Africa could not have brought down apartheid on its own. But it did help Black Africa to maintain pressure on South Africa. It produced difficulties between South Africa and other countries who may not have liked racial segregation but who nevertheless kept up normal diplomatic and trading links with South Africa. Apartheid was kept on the front as well as the back pages. By the mid 1980s pressure for change was building up from inside South Africa and that raised the question of economic sanctions.

Most athletes worldwide and most sports officials just wanted to play. They talked of 'keeping politics out of sport' and 'building bridges'. They were always detecting improvements in South Africa. Black political activists, on the other hand, did not want to see integrated sport. How could sport be integrated if the rest of society was segregated? Recent changes in the apartheid laws in 1991 were welcomed by the International Olympic Committee, the International Cricket Council and the International Rugby Board. South Africa took part in the Cricket World Cup in Australia in 1992 and sent a multi-racial team to the Barcelona Olympics. But whites have long enjoyed much higher living standards than blacks and better facilities for sport. Until those things change uncertainties about South Africa will continue.

Sport and Nationalism

Sport has been mixed up with national identities ever since the modern sporting world began. Many Scots for example used the football matches with England to parade their Scottishness, their separateness from the English. A small nation, like Scotland, can occasionally succeed on the sports field against a larger nation which dominates it in other parts of life. The Welsh use their rugby prowess, especially in matches against England, in the same way. In Spain, football matches between Barcelona and Real Madrid have come to represent the Catalan-speaking north-east against the

Madrid-dominated Spanish Government.

The role of cricket in the West Indies has worked in a similar way. In the nineteenth century, British rule brought trade, the English language and cricket to the West Indies. Cricket gave the black man the chance to play with the white man and eventually to demonstrate that he could do it better than his colonial master. Since 1928, the performance of West Indian cricketers has achieved the widest recognition for Barbados, Guyana, Jamaica and Trinidad, especially among ordinary people in the English-speaking world

The great West Indian cricketer, Viv Richards, is widely recognised and admired throughout the English-speaking world. Sport can have a uniting influence: the idea of the 'West Indies' mainly comes alive in the cricket team.

outside North America. However, Jamaica is separated from the countries of the Eastern Caribbean by a thousand miles of ocean. They have different ways of life and different interests compared to Guyana and Trinidad. The West Indian cricket team functions as a coherent unit but an attempt to set up a political federation when the British left failed. It is true that there are regional economic institutions to which the individual countries belong but the idea of the West Indies mainly comes alive in their cricket team.

Sport can help to form national identity and it has often been used by new nations both to help build such feelings at home and to gain prestige and recognition abroad. East Germany was an excellent example of such a process. With a young population the Communist Government decided to invest its limited resources in the major Olympic sports. Eventually 9,000 coaches, 14 special sports schools, a special sports university at Leipzig, training camps, indoor tracks and sports medicine clinics combined in a relentless pursuit of athletic excellence. The results were seen at many major sporting events between 1968 and 1990.

Communist Cuba did something similar. They wanted to show the world that their economic and political system worked: it produced the best athletes, it made the people proud to be Cubans. Cuba says sport is political: sporting heroes have a duty to the Revolution and society. For instance, Cuban pride in boxer Téofilo Stevenson, twice winner of the heavyweight gold medal in the Olympics, was supported by the assertion that he was an ordinary worker and a deputy in the national assembly. Interestingly, Cuba has become the most successful sporting nation in Latin America even though it has one of the smallest populations.

Fidel Castro, the Cuban leader, playing baseball.

Sport has also been used to promote nation-building in Africa. It does not always work. Tribal, ethnic and local loyalties remain and are often reflected in sport. Inter-ethnic rivalry has produced football violence in Cameroon and Nigeria. In Tanzania, the success of big-city teams from Dar Es Salaam has led to resentment in rural districts and obstructed the unifying function of sport.

Governments try to associate themselves with sporting success. President Kennedy began the practice of ringing up the winners of the American Superbowl to congratulate them. Military regimes in Argentina and Brazil exploited the World Cup victories of 1978 and 1970. The footballer, Pele, has been exploited by successive Brazilian Governments as a national resource. It would be no surprise if he ran for President himself.

Sport is part of society. Sport is part of international relations. It can be used to support any political claim or philosophy. It cannot avoid being mixed up with politics in spite of the fact that many players and administrators complain about it. Sport can certainly influence national feeling but it is unlikely to be a cause of one country's hostility to another. In 1969, Honduras and El Salvador went to war for five days after a World Cup match, but quarrels between the two countries already existed over other issues. The hostility would still be there if the football was not. The niggling question is, does sport make things worse?

6 Sport and science

One of the frustrations suffered by sports enthusiasts is that there seems to be no objective way of comparing the stars of the present to those of the past. How would Australian batsman Don Bradman have coped with today's West Indies fast bowlers? Would French tennis champion, Suzanne Lenglen, have been able to beat today's outstanding players such as Steffi Graf or Monica Seles? How would the great English footballer, Stanley Matthews, have fared against the defences of modern-day Liverpool or AC Milan? Would the undefeated heavyweight champion of the 1950s, Rocky Marciano, have knocked out Mike Tyson, or would it have been the other way round? Such unknowables provide endless opportunities for speculation and argument.

In some sports, however, achievement and performance can be measured precisely because in certain cases we know how fast athletes ran, how far they threw, how high they jumped, how fast they swam. We can make comparisons of performance over time. Johnny Weismuller was the first actor to play Tarzan on the screen. Before that, he had swum for the United States in the Olympics of 1924 and 1928. His time for the 100 metres freestyle in 1924 was beaten by the winner of the women's event at the Munich Olympics in 1972. Even more spectacularly, his 1924 winning time for the 400 metres freestyle would not have qualified him for either the men's or the women's finals in 1972.

Between 1896 and 1976, the time for the men's 100 metre sprint in athletics improved by 16.2 per cent and for the 1,500 metres by almost 20 per cent.

No one had run a mile in less than four minutes until Roger Bannister did so in 1954: since then many hundreds of individuals have done it on countless occasions.

There is no single explanation for these improvements. Better food, health and social welfare generally may have helped athletes improve their performance. They may also have been encouraged by the growing financial and status rewards available from sport. However, a further important factor is that there is now a more scientific attitude to training and to preparation for performance. This has not only helped to increase body strength, speed and stamina but it has led to improvements in technique in some events. Science has been increasingly applied to sport and even in Britain there are now professors in sports science.

The main base subjects of this growing area of study are physiology, biomechanics, psychology and nutrition. Work in these areas has meant that we know more about how the athlete's body works than ever before.

Physiology

Exercise physiology has a long history but it was first seriously applied to the task of producing athletic champions in the Soviet Union and East Germany, particularly after the Second World War. Research was also stimulated by the decision of the International Olympic Committee to award the 1968 Games to Mexico City. Mexico City is about 7,000 feet (2,000 metres) above sea level. At such a high altitude there is less oxygen and there was anxiety that this would favour those athletes who usually lived and trained at such levels. It was also known that the thin air would produce difficulties in the longer-distance races, all of which were, in fact, won by athletes brought up at high altitudes.

Research designed to understand the way in which muscles contract and how they respond to sustained effort has suggested that athletes vary in their physiological types. Some – the sprinters – are best suited to running very fast over short distances. They are born with a higher proportion of fast muscle fibres which take 0.07 of a second to contract. They are less dependent on oxygen to release energy from glucose in food. Special training programmes can be worked out to increase the area of fast muscle fibre. Athletes with this type of metabolism tend to produce more lactic acid in the muscles, which makes them tire quickly. Other sports where players move in short sharp bursts – like football – are also best suited to those with fast muscle fibres. English footballer Gary Lineker, for example, is almost certain to have a high proportion of this type of muscle.

Those athletes with a high proportion of slow muscle fibres are best fitted for events and sports which demand endurance over longer periods rather than moments of short, sharp action. Slow muscle fibres take twice or three times as long to contract as fast ones. They require plenty of oxygen to release energy from glucose or fat. Scientists can measure an individual athlete's capacity to take in oxygen. For top long-distance runners, for example, that capacity has to be high.

If the aim is to increase overall muscle strength (for shot putters, for example), then the training would be designed to increase the size of all the muscle fibres. Better blood circulation inside the muscles should result, increasing the oxygen supply and the number of enzymes which release energy using that oxygen.

By assessing the physiological make-up of individuals, scientists can advise them and their coaches on what the best form of training

Physiology

Physiology means simply the study of the natural physical world. Human physiology studies how the systems of the body function and interact. This also involves understanding the structure of the body. For example, to study the physiology of exercise one might have to study the respiratory system, as well as the structure of bone, cartilage, tendons and muscles.

would be. Perhaps some day the exact strengths and weaknesses of sportsplayers will be pinpointed in the laboratory but is this progress to be welcomed?

Sport and science.

Biomechanics

Many sports demand a high level of technical skill before much can be achieved. Biomechanics can help improve a sportsperson's technique, and the practitioners of this science study movement in two main ways:

- *Electro-mechanical*. The pressure which an athlete puts on the ground, and his or her velocity and acceleration, can be measured using what are known as force plates.
- *Optical*. The movement of sportsmen and sportswomen can be photographed with sophisticated cameras which produce 500 picture frames per second (as opposed to the 24 frames per second of the normal video or cine camera). The result is a much more accurate picture, which enables the movement of the individual to be analysed in the most microscopic detail.

Like physiology, biomechanics is yet another aid for the discovery of the exact strengths and weaknesses of an individual athlete. Indeed the most up-to-date equipment, such as that housed in the new biomechanical work station at University College Salford, can take pictures of human movement via a computer which translates the pictures into stick figures. This allows a most detailed examination of stride patterns and stride lengths, and up to four movement sequences can be examined at the same time. 'Normal' and 'abnormal' functions can be looked for and studies made of athletes before and after medical treatment.

Biomechanicians stress that their work not only helps the small minority of top sporting figures but can also be used to help people with walking difficulties, such as those who have had hip replacement operations. The difficult question is: Who should get priority?

Psychology

Stress and strain in sport, as in other walks of life, are not only physical: they are also found in the mind. The South African golfer, Gary Player, once said that winning was over 90 per cent in the mind. In top-level sport there may be some truth in this. Certainly there is a good deal of evidence to suggest that the difference between performing well and badly is a psychological one.

One of the main ways in which the psychologist can support sportsplayers is by helping them to conquer pre-competition nerves. One normal consequence of this sort of anxiety is the familiar 'butterflies' in the stomach. However, the mind may become over-anxious, resulting in psychological problems as well as physical symptoms such as cramp in the muscles. Anxiety is often dealt with by meditation: if the mind can relax, then relaxation of the body will follow. If the tension is more muscular, then muscle-relaxing exercises are used and, if they work, a more relaxed attitude should result.

Psychology

Psychology is the study of mind and behaviour. Sports psychologists try to improve the mental attitudes and techniques of sportsplayers. To perform at their best they need to be neither too excited nor too laid back, but at an 'optimum level of arousal'. This means they will be more likely to read the game better, and will also be more confident.

Mental skills, such as how to relax and how to think positively about performing, need to be practised just like physical skills. Most leading sportsplayers include a sports psychologist as part of their training team.

Sports psychologists are interested in helping athletes in other ways too, in particular by getting them to concentrate better. Controlling the attention is important: the aim is to focus all the senses and all the thoughts on the game or event, to the exclusion of everything else. Psychologists claim that they can also improve people's motivation and self-confidence. They try to train sportsplayers to use their imaginations more effectively: to step outside themselves, for example, and watch their performance in their mind's eye. They believe that if you can imagine performing well, then you can do it. This kind of work may prove to be more successful with individual sports than with team sports.

Finally, evidence is beginning to mount up that particular physiological types have a psychological make-up to match. Marathon runners with slow muscle fibres may tend to have dogged, stubborn personalities. They may tend to be shy and quiet, but they may also possess the determination needed for those 26 miles and 385 yards. Will every major sportsman and sportswoman one day have a psychologist as well as a coach?

Behaviour	Comments	Countdown to performance
Wake up	Smile. Say, 'Today's the day.'	7.45 a.m.
Eat a leisurely breakfast	Cereal, toast and honey, coffee. Say, 'I feel good.'	8.00
Shave/shower		8.30
Get dressed	Shoes, not trainers. Smart, confident.	8.45
Check kit	Remember spike key and new spikes	9.00
Leave for competition	Have one final look in the mirror. Say, 'I look the business.' Spring in stride. Buy newspaper.	9.15
On journey	Sit down as much as possible. Listen to music, read paper.	
Confirm time of event with coach		
Mental rehearsal of warm-up and jumps	Slow and thorough	4 hours

An example of a pre-competition routine for a triple jumper. Athletes are encouraged to design a programme for total preparation before an event. Routines should be specific enough to be reproduced time after time.

Eat lunch	High in carbohydrate	3 hours
Arrive at venue. Look at track layout, check pit, board distance, runway, bounce	'I'm here and it feels good.'	90 minutes
Get changed, go to toilet		75 minutes
Begin warm-up – 800m jog, stretching routine	Methodical progression through body	50 minutes
Striding/bouncing. Full speed, measure run-up and mark	Pick up tempo. Think 'power' and 'floating'	30 minutes
Practice run-throughs	Focus on technique	10 minutes
Report in. Check order and position		5 minutes
Sit down. Mental rehearsal of first jump	Think 'power' and 'floating'	2 minutes
Stand up. Vigorous stretching, pumping actions	Think 'pump up'. Get excited	1 minute
Get ready as previous jumper begins	Get angry, emotional	30 seconds
Tee-shirt off, then bottoms. Touch toes, double-footed vertical spring	'Come on now!'	
Foot on marker, head up, eyes fixed	Wait for wind to drop	10 seconds
Visualise the jump GO!	See a big one	0 seconds

Nutrition

The pleasures of eating and drinking have to be enjoyed in moderation by the serious sportsplayer. The nutritionist is yet another member of the back-up team which sport has taken from science. There are no magic recipes for success, of course, but expert advice can be offered on what to eat, when to eat and how much to eat. Diet programmes can be planned for the individual athlete, whose needs may differ depending on which sport they practise. Triathletes' dietary needs will differ from those of discus throwers, for example, and a golfer's diet should be different from a footballer's. Again, the aim is to use the latest research to improve performance. There is no simple diet for sport: the subject remains hemmed in by fads and fancies. Nutritionists often tell their sporting clients to eat sensibly, cut down on fats, eat more carbohydrates and less confectionery. Between 50 and 60 per cent of the calories we need should come from carbohydrates, but from cereals and bread, and *not* from sweets, cakes and chocolate.

Another vital person for the sportsplayer today: the dietitian. Diet has been found to make a real difference to an athlete's performance – natural talent, training and mental approach are not enough.

How much do you know about nutrition? This is an extract from a quiz which helps correct misinformation.

NUTRITION QUIZ

1   In general the diet that provides the best performance for the athlete is a variety of foods providing energy from carbohydrate, protein and fat in the following percentages:
- (a) 75%, 15%, 10%
- (b) 30–40%, 25–35%, 25–45%
- (c) 55–60%, 10–15%, 25–30%
- (d) 40%, 30%, 20%

2   Protein intake in excess of needs is:
- (a) converted to muscle
- (b) used as energy
- (c) excreted by the body
- (d) stored as body fat

3   Which of the following is the most readily available source of food energy?
- (a) carbohydrate
- (b) protein
- (c) fat
- (d) vitamins

4   Which of the following is the most concentrated source of food energy?
- (a) dietary fibre
- (b) alcohol
- (c) fat
- (d) sugar

5   What is glycogen?
- (a) the storage form of protein
- (b) adipose tissue
- (c) a muscle stimulant
- (d) the storage form of carbohydrate

6   Which provides quick energy if taken immediately before a short term event?
- (a) glucose, honey
- (b) spaghetti
- (c) orange juice
- (d) none of the above

7   What is the safest way to increase muscle mass?
- (a) increase muscle work
- (b) increase protein intake
- (c) take vitamin and mineral supplements
- (d) take anabolic steroid drugs

8   Approximately how much water can the body lose through sweating before salt replacement is required?
- (a) 4 litres
- (b) 6 litres
- (c) 1 litre
- (d) 2 litres

9   What is the best fluid to drink during competition?
- (a) commercial electrolyte replacement drinks
- (b) water
- (c) unsweetened fruit juices
- (d) cordial

10 Are salt tablets necessary?
- (a) yes, for endurance events
- (b) yes, if weight has been lost during competition
- (c) no, they may cause nausea, vomiting, dizziness
- (d) none of the above

Answers
1 (c); 2 (d); 3 (a); 4 (c); 5 (d); 6 (d); 7 (a); 8 (a); 9 (b); 10 (c)

Sports medicine

We shall reserve our discussion of the role of pharmacology (drugs) in sport for the next chapter. In this one we have been concentrating on those sciences which have been legitimately used by sports practitioners to improve performance. Sports medicine also plays an increasingly important role in sport by sometimes curing, sometimes alleviating, the pain and damage which sportsmen and sportswomen inflict on themselves and each other. Sports medicine is one of the fastest-growing specialities in healthcare in Britain. There is a British Association of Sport and Medicine which promotes research and training courses. Under the auspices of the Society of Public Health, the fifth annual Sports Medicine Conference was held in 1990. An amazing range of issues was discussed from chronic badminton injuries and thrower's and server's shoulder to 'aggressive diagnosis in sport' and laser therapy in sports medicine.

The price of playing on: Manchester United and England footballer, Bryan Robson, has a long history of injury. The pressure to play while injured – from team managers and the players themselves – is very strong but long-term injuries can be the result.

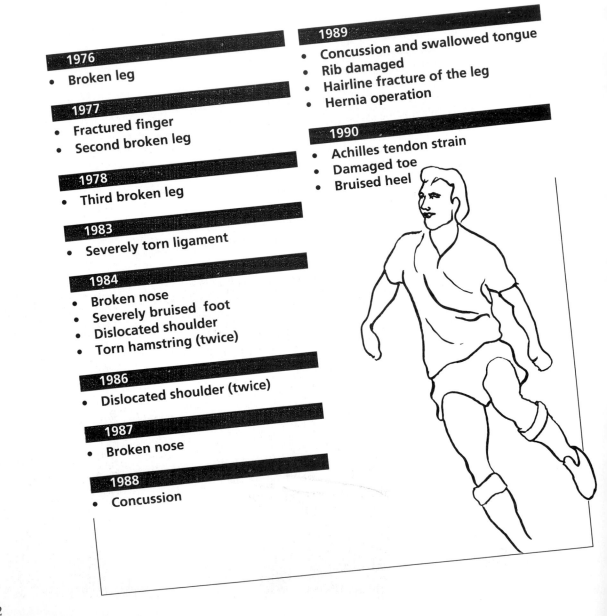

1976
- Broken leg

1977
- Fractured finger
- Second broken leg

1978
- Third broken leg

1983
- Severely torn ligament

1984
- Broken nose
- Severely bruised foot
- Dislocated shoulder
- Torn hamstring (twice)

1986
- Dislocated shoulder (twice)

1987
- Broken nose

1988
- Concussion

1989
- Concussion and swallowed tongue
- Rib damaged
- Hairline fracture of the leg
- Hernia operation

1990
- Achilles tendon strain
- Damaged toe
- Bruised heel

Getting the sportsplayer back on the field after injury has become big business. For the professionals, of course, the pressure to play while not fully fit, to use modern sprays and injections to conceal the pain, is very great. Amateurs often do not allow themselves enough recovery time after injury either: the body has a considerable capacity to heal itself provided it is given the chance and not giving it the chance may lead to the eventual abandonment of a favourite sport and a long period of inconvenience and pain. The Arthritis and Rheumatism Council for Research issues a free pamphlet to guide people with sports injuries. All sportsplayers should read it.

Sports medicine plays an increasingly important role in keeping the top sports shows on the road, but the doctor's advice may not always be taken. Too many players are forced to play on when they should be resting. Look at the effect that all-the-year-round physical effort over several years has had on the British rugby league star, Ellery Hanley, the Argentinian footballer, Diego Maradona, and the English footballer, Bryan Robson. And when medical science fails ...? The England football captain flew a faith healer to Italy during the 1990 World Cup in the hope of improving his injured achilles tendon.

Technology

Technology

Technology is the practical application of science. No modern sportsplayer is unaffected by technology. It has changed the clothes in which they play, the equipment they play with and the surfaces they play on. Technology has helped the athlete to train harder, ride, run and swim faster, jump higher and throw further.

Sport as spectacle has been transformed by technology. No longer is it limited to the daylight and out-of-doors. Moreover, television and communications satellites make it possible for a worldwide audience to share the same spectacle at the exact moment it happens.

Technology has clearly helped shape the development of many modern sports and events. Railways and steamships helped the spread of sports across continents in the nineteenth century. Airlines have made even more frequent the number of days the sporting circus can be in town. The role of television has been considered in chapter four.

A spectacular evolution: pole vaulters go higher and higher, as technology advances.
A pole vaulter using a wooden pole, London, 1872.

On the field or on the track, artificial all-weather surfaces have made play possible in places where it would not have been possible before. They have helped runners to go faster than they could on the old cinder tracks. Javelins go further now that aerodynamics has been applied to their design. As technological innovations rapidly increase, motor sport – on both two and four wheels – is continually threatening to burst the bounds of the driver's ability to control the machine. Moreover, all these faster times can be accurately registered on the most sensitive photo-timing equipment ever known.

Not all of these changes have been welcomed. Artificial pitches do not behave like grass. Footballers, for example, dislike the high bounce and the burn injuries. Similarly, the larger metal tennis racket, with its larger 'sweet spot' which makes it easier to hit the ball, has encouraged power at the expense of finesse. In the women's game especially, it has allowed children to compete on equal terms with adults. Some critics have said that unlimited racquet power is making tennis less interesting to watch.

The Soviet pole vaulter, Sergei Bubka, European champion in 1988, using a fibre pole.

Reaching your peak?

There are at least 52 degree courses in British universities and polytechnics in the general area of physical education, and most have a base in sports science. There are a further 57 courses in colleges of higher education. There are many more in countries such as the USA, Canada, Germany and Australia. The world's first diploma in science and football is claimed by Liverpool Polytechnic (now the Liverpool John Moores University). It is no longer only the countries of Eastern Europe who take sports science seriously.

We have seen that sports science comprises several disciplines and we have also seen the direct impact that those disciplines have on sport. In particular, scientists and coaches have come together to try to help sportsmen and sportswomen do their best when it matters most. Reaching the peak of performance during an Olympic Games or a World Championship has become the aim of each athlete, coach and scientific adviser. Training is built up around periods of great effort and periods of lesser intensity, but the effort needed is gradually increased to ever higher levels followed by rest periods. In this way the body is given the opportunity to adapt to each new load placed upon it and the new muscle strengths become the norm! However, a few weeks before the competition, training is relaxed – not too much or else the new levels of strength, speed and stamina will be eroded – but enough to allow physical and psychological recovery. Finding the right moment when the athlete is physically and mentally in his or her peak condition may be as much art as science – the East Germans seem to have been especially good at it – but science has certainly provided more knowledge about how to identify that moment.

There is, however, a bigger question about the relationship between science and sport. How far should scientific knowledge be applied to making winners? Where should the line be drawn and by whom? If athletes can be biochemically reprogrammed, does it matter? Will transplants of key tissue or organs become a commonplace of sports medicine? Will nervomuscular electrical stimulation be used to make athletes faster and stronger? Is it possible that in some sports, competition between laboratories will be as intense as between athletes? Science cannot help us to grapple with the meanings of sport. It cannot help us to appreciate a good pass in football, a good stroke by the tennis player, a great catch by the baseball outfielder. Not everything can be measured but in the light of what we already know about the nature of scientific progress, the world of sport may soon be faced by more hard questions.

7 Drugs and sport

Canadian athlete, Ben Johnson, at the start of the 100 metre final at the Seoul Olympics, 1988. Three days after his victory in the race, he was stripped of his gold medal after failing a drug test. Should sportsmen and women be allowed to take drugs? How serious is the problem and how should sport deal with the issue?

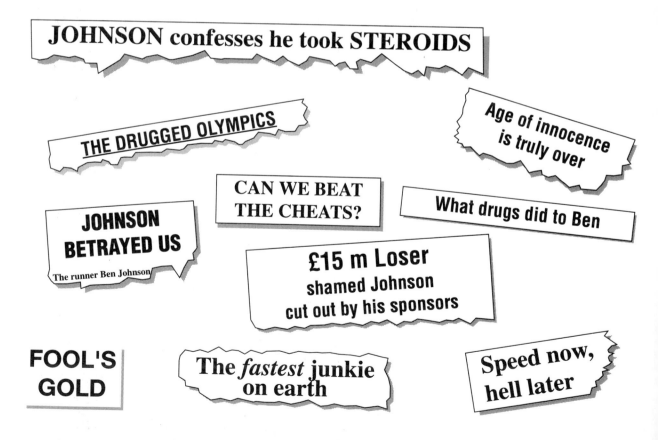

JOHNSON confesses he took STEROIDS

THE DRUGGED OLYMPICS

Age of innocence is truly over

JOHNSON BETRAYED US

The runner Ben Johnson

CAN WE BEAT THE CHEATS?

What drugs did to Ben

£15 m Loser
shamed Johnson
cut out by his sponsors

FOOL'S GOLD

The *fastest* junkie on earth

Speed now, hell later

In 1988, Ben Johnson became the first Olympic gold medal winner to be stripped of his title after failing a drug test. Three days before, he had not only won Olympic Gold at Seoul, but had become the first man to break his own world record in the 100 metres. Now both medal and world record were gone. Seoul and the world of sport, as every newspaper and television station round the globe proclaimed to readers and viewers, was in a state of shock.

The reverberations of that moment were continuing nine months later and not only in Johnson's adopted country, Canada, where a Royal Commission of Inquiry was investigating 'the use of drugs and banned practices intended to increase athletic performances'. In Australia there was a parliamentary inquiry into the use of drugs in sport and the subject was also discussed at a meeting of European Sports Ministers. It seemed that Ben Johnson's exposure had finally brought a new urgency to the question of what sport should do about its drug problem.

Drugs are a part of everyone's everyday life. Not only are they used to treat a variety of illnesses from flu to heart disease, but more generally they are used for the following purposes:

- to relieve pain
- to remove anxiety
- to bring on sleep
- to fend sleep off
- to put on weight

Drugs are also used in and for recreation. Some of these, like cocaine and marijuana, are illegal in many countries. Others, like alcohol and tobacco, are not. The central question for sport is whether sportsmen and sportswomen should be allowed to take drugs to improve their performance. The arguments against drug use usually involve five main points:

- Taking drugs to improve performance undermines the whole idea of sport, which depends on the competition being honest. Everyone should have the same chance.
- Sport is often praised as an aid to health. Drug-taking, which is not medically prescribed, almost certainly undermines health, if not in the present, then in the future.
- Athletes are young and therefore inexperienced and vulnerable to the pressures which might be put on them by coaches, sponsors, administrators and even governments. They need protection.
- Drugs which build up feelings of aggression may have anti-social effects off as well as on the field.
- Sports personalities should set an example to their fans. Even recreational drug-taking may encourage emulation by young supporters with damaging individual and social results.

Why do athletes take drugs?

Top sport has become the victim of its own success. Successful sports stars can earn huge amounts either from advertisers, sponsors or governments. The media and the public seem determined to give to sport an importance which puts extra pressure on those who take part. Physical strain, not surprisingly, leads the competitor to look for all the help he or she can get. It is tempting to turn to drugs, and

'I've had that. Where's the baton?'

Professional cycling has long had the reputation of being associated with drug abuse. A rider in the Tour de France has to keep to such a punishing race programme that he requires 8,000 calories a day just to keep him in the saddle. Normally, a man requires about 2,000 calories a day.

tempting for coaches, doctors and trainers to suggest it.

Many successful track and field athletes receive large sums in trust funds rather than having jobs as was usual in the past. They go to warm climates to train and sometimes go to high altitudes in an attempt to improve their performance. Some see no moral difference between that kind of action and taking a pill or having an injection.

Some people would argue that sportsplayers have little choice. If competitors suspect that their rivals take drugs, they may feel pressured into doing the same. They may argue that it is up to each individual to decide. The risk to health, especially of using mixtures of drugs and of taking large doses, will be taken by the individual athlete. The risk of being found out will also be taken by individuals. Ben Johnson, for example, passed 17 drug tests after races in 1986 and 1987 even though he was taking steroids throughout those years.

No one knows what proportion of sportsmen and sportswomen have used drugs to improve their performances. In the last 25 years there have been a few spectacular cases and a lot of allegations and rumours. During most of this period, testing was patchy, with many organisations refusing to set up testing schemes because they claimed drug-taking did not take place in their sports. Many of the testing schemes which were used were relatively easy to avoid, often because they took place during competitions and, by then, athletes had usually removed any detectable traces of drugs. In Britain, the Sports Council had to threaten to withdraw grants from governing bodies of sports who refused to introduce random tests in both training and competition.

Random testing was first carried out on British track and field athletes in 1986/87. 'Random' meant that an athlete's name was taken from a list and he or she was told 48 hours in advance that they were going to be tested. Some experts argued that this was long enough to enable a guilty athlete to use another drug – a masking agent – to cover traces of earlier ones. In 1986/87, 164 tests on 134 athletes produced no positive results, although six athletes refused to be tested and retired from sport.

The effectiveness of the scheme was challenged in *The Times*, where it was claimed that some British officials had helped competitors at international meetings to avoid tests. An inquiry into the extent of drug abuse in British athletics in 1988 suggested that 10 per cent of athletes probably took drugs. By then the Sports Council had introduced random, out-of-season testing covering about thirty sports in which drug abuse was thought to be present.

The Royal Commission in Canada, set up after the Johnson case, has provided information from other athletes. Canada's leading woman sprinter, Angella Issajenko, quoted from a diary in which she had kept details of both her training and her drug-taking over a ten-year period. It was an essential part of her athletic equipment along with a book about drugs and 18 hypodermic needles.

What drugs do sportsplayers take?

Stimulants
The aim of those who have taken these drugs has been to increase alertness and physical endurance. The most well known stimulants are amphetamines, often called 'pep pills' or 'speed'. Their effect is to increase the heart rate, respiration and blood pressure and to stimulate the brain. They produce feelings of confidence and euphoria. High doses can have unpleasant side-effects and stimulants tend to be very addictive, like cocaine. The body develops a tolerance of the drug so that increasing amounts have to be taken to achieve the same effect.

The National Football League in America banned amphetamines in 1971. Some players were taking them before every match, especially those in key defensive roles – the ends and the blockers – and high doses were producing hostile and aggressive behaviour as well as diminishing the feeling of pain. The League has still not introduced a drug-testing scheme even though there have been allegations that 40 per cent of the players take cocaine. The players claim such tests would infringe their individual rights.

Depressants
The purpose of this group of drugs is to reduce tension. They are thought to be especially useful in those sports requiring a steady hand, such as archery, darts, fencing, golf, shooting and snooker.

The sporting bodies for cycling have brought in a system of strict controls and stringent penalties, which is helping to eradicate the use of drugs by cyclists.

In 1967, the British cyclist, Tommy Simpson, died during the Tour de France. The cause of death was heart failure due to heat exhaustion. He had been taking amphetamines which had concealed his growing exhaustion.

Alcohol and smoking both have the effect of calming the nerves and neither is banned by the International Olympic Committee, although the blood alcohol level of fencers, for example, must not be above 50 mg per 100 ml. This compares with 80 mg per 100 ml for car drivers in Britain.

Informed estimates suggested that almost a quarter of all competitors in the 1972 Olympic pentathlon used tranquillisers for the shooting events. Modern drugs such as beta blockers further complicate the picture. They are used to treat heart disorders and high blood pressure but they also have the effect of relaxing those who take them. They have not been banned by the IOC. At the 1984 Olympics, however, competitors in the pentathlon had to produce a doctor's certificate stating that they needed to take them for health reasons. Team managers offered certificates covering whole teams! Some snooker players have had beta blockers prescribed by doctors. This has caused controversy in a sport which requires a steady cue arm.

Muscle builders

Anabolic steroids have become the most notorious group of drugs. They were developed after the Second World War and are used by doctors to aid growth after serious illness. They increase body weight. It is not clear when they were first used by sportsplayers, but body-builders and weight-lifters in the United States and the Soviet Union were certainly using them from the early 1960s.

Anabolic steroids: unfair competition.

Soon after, they were taken up by some athletes in the strength events of shot-putting, hammer-throwing and discus. Between 1956 and 1972 the average weight of shot-putters in the Olympics rose by 14 per cent. Steroids were banned by the IOC's Medical Commission in 1975.

In spite of this, steroid use had spread to the runners by the end of the 1970s. In 1979, three female 1,500 metre runners were banned after positive tests at the Balkan Games. In 1983, after eleven weight-lifters had been disqualified from the Pan-American Games, 13 American track and field athletes returned home without competing.

Experts seem to agree that steroids make longer and harder training periods possible. They also help athletes to recover from competition and training more quickly so that they can do more of both. Some athletes clearly believe that steroids make them run faster or throw further. If they know that they are getting bigger, that probably boosts confidence and attainment. It was one of this group of drugs which Ben Johnson was found guilty of taking in Seoul.

Steroids are also believed to increase aggression. In 1985, the American magazine *Sports Illustrated* suggested that 75 per cent of American Football players in the National Football League were regular users.

Another muscle-building drug that has been available since the mid 1970s is the male hormone, testosterone. This is produced naturally in men, making testing more complicated as the authorities have to calculate what are normal and abnormal levels.

There is some concern about the side-effects of steroids, which can be alarming. For women, they can lead to the growth of facial hair, a deepening voice, and the disappearance of breasts. The appearance of men can also be changed by regular steroid use. In men, breasts may develop and they may become impotent. The longer-term effects may not be clear for some time yet, although there have been cases of kidney and liver tumours and deaths following large and regular doses of steroids.

Painkillers

As we have seen, sportsplayers are becoming actively involved at a younger age and are training longer and harder than in the past. This is true of many who will never reach the elite and those who do get close to the top feel they must go through rigorous training programmes if they are to become winners in modern sport. It means that they are putting enormous pressure on their bodies and particularly on their joints, ligaments, muscles and tendons. Many players become obsessional about training and practice and this can lead to overuse injuries. In turn it tempts them to resort to pain-relieving drugs to avoid having to stop training or miss important competitions for which they have been preparing for a long time. Suppressing pain by sprays or drugs can be dangerous. Like the old cold sponge of the football club trainer, modern sprays produce a rapid cooling of the skin which provides temporary relief, but can hide underlying problems.

There is evidence that some boxers and cyclists have used heroin and morphine for the combination of additional stimulation and lessening of pain which they provide. It has been asserted that during the 1986 World Amateur Boxing championships in Reno, the members of the Cuban team took lidocaine, a painkiller not on the IOC's banned list.

This list of banned substances seems destined to grow ever longer as work in the laboratory, funded and exploited by companies or governments, continues to produce substances or techniques which try to outwit the testers. Growth hormones and diuretics which promote urine production and which may help to expel other drugs from the system are two relatively recent additions to the sportsman's kitbag. So is the technique of blood doping. This involves the withdrawal and later reintroduction of red blood cells in order to increase the oxygen-carrying capacity of the blood, and therefore the quantity of oxygen available to the muscle. In 1985 it was revealed that several members of the American cycling team had undergone this operation before the Los Angeles Olympics in 1984. They won nine medals.

What is to be done?

It is clear that there is no simple solution but there are three areas in which the campaign against drugs in sport must be fought.

Testing and controls

Testing is feasible and it does work both in deterring some and in exposing others. But it needs to be carried out randomly and at any time. It also requires co-operation at the international level so that no sportsman or sportswoman in one country can feel disadvantaged by knowing that those in another country can escape drug controls. It is a costly burden that contemporary sport everywhere must bear. About 4,500 tests a year take place in Britain alone. Should some of the profits from the Olympics made by the IOC help to pay for them?

Punishment

Former British athlete Sebastian Coe and others have argued for life bans on those found guilty of taking banned drugs. The practice has often been very different. Ilona Slupaniek won the gold medal in the shot-put at the European Championships in 1978. She then failed a drug test and lost the medal, but was reinstated and came back to win the Olympic title at Moscow in 1980. Ben Johnson only suffered a two-year ban.

Again, banning has to be international. That probably means agreement and co-operation not just between sporting organisations but between governments. The improvement of East–West relations should help this process.

Education

This must be an equally important part of any attack on the use of drugs in sport. Zoë Warwicke became a British national champion body-builder but she took drugs, including steroids, for one year to help her to do it. It cost her £100 a week and caused her serious health problems. She believes that athletes should be taught about drugs, starting at school. She does not believe that fines or bans are an effective deterrent as they merely stimulate the black market for drugs. They do, however, encourage those sportsmen and sportswomen who want fair competition.

Perhaps the public need educating too. They need to be persuaded, in all countries, to change their perspective on sport. Foul play should be ruled out, and taking drugs is foul play.

8 Sport for all?

Is sport good for the body?

A total of 11 million people go swimming in Britain each week. Asia has 54 million registered football players. Sport really is a worldwide activity which can be followed and appreciated by all kinds of people in all nations.

Sport for all: American Chad Colley on his way to a gold medal at the 5th Paralympics held in France in 1992.

Unesco

United Nations Educational, Scientific and Cultural Organisation: an agency of the United Nations that sponsors programmes to promote education, the arts, sport etc.

Is 'Sport for All' either possible or desirable? The slogan was adopted as official policy by all those governments which made up the Council of Europe in 1966. The Sports Council in Britain launched its own campaign for 'Sport for All' in 1972 and many non-European countries have since done the same.

The slogan did not mean that everyone should play some sport, nor, even, that everyone wanted to play sport – most people have little or no interest in it. What the slogan *did* mean was that everyone ought to take part in some form of regular physical activity. It could be fitness training, dance, yoga or jogging, or it could be a sport like cricket, basketball, badminton or cycling.

A Unesco report in 1980 showed that the aim of most 'Sport for All' programmes was to improve the health of the population. Regular exercise will not prevent heart disease but there is a clear association between heart disease and lack of exercise. Putting the heart and lungs to work for three 15 minute sessions a week, either walking, cycling, jogging or swimming, can help improve your body and make you feel better.

Sport, on the other hand, is not necessarily good for you. It may be one of the pleasures of the flesh, but it can certainly do the flesh some damage. Injuries are the bane of the professional athlete. Baseball pitchers and tennis players get bad elbows, American footballers and rugby players get block-tackled into hospital. The

73

knees and ankles of soccer players become arthritic and their legs get broken. Runners suffer from stress fractures and strained muscles and all sportsmen and sportswomen are vulnerable to back trouble. Top athletes are not always healthier than non-athletes.

Fair play, fellowship and enjoyment?

Sport can inflict forms of damage other than the physical. The Olympic motto seems harmless enough: *Citius, Altius, Fortius* – Faster, Higher, Stronger. But does it mean faster, higher and stronger than anyone else? It is a small step from that to believing in prize-winning above everything else. In professional sport the pressure to win puts a strain on the integrity of players, coaches and administrators. Vince Lombardi, coach of the American football team Green Bay Packers in the 1960s, once said: 'Winning isn't everything; it's the only thing.' He also said: 'There is nothing that stokes the fires like a dose of hatred.'

Is it only the result that matters and the result that is played for? At top-level sport it frequently seems that it is and this attitude is often imitated by the lesser players. Such ruthlessness makes a mockery of the Olympic movement, with its aim 'to educate young people through sport in a spirit of better understanding between each other and of friendship'. It also undermines all those other qualities that sport has long been associated with – fair play, fellowship and enjoyment.

Over exposure?

Even if sport were definitely a 'good thing' it could be argued that there is too much of it: every second year there is either World Cup football or the Olympics, and world championships are commonplace. Many sports events are increasingly shaped for television's apparently insatiable appetite. So many of the big sports gatherings have become 'swollen carnivals'. Is world football really shown to the best advantage by a tournament which lasts a month and consists of 52 matches? There were only 17 Olympic sports in 1960 – why had this number risen to 25 by 1992?

Professional sport seems to have become dominated by business and is heading down a road to monotony and homogenisation. Football styles, for example, used to reflect the kind of lifestyle and temperament of the different countries who played the game. In the 1990 World Cup, all the teams looked virtually the same, apart from their shirt colours. Sport has become part of a world in which people consume and conform.

A male terrain?

Sport has also been a traditionally masculine terrain, one of the ways in which men have kept themselves apart from women in general, and wives and families in particular. Both playing and watching sport has been mainly for men.

There was powerful opposition to the participation of women in the Olympics. Although they officially competed for the first time in 1908, there was no athletics programme for women until 1928 and then there were only five events – the 100 and 800 metres, the long jump, the discus and the 400 metre hurdles. Moreover, some female competitors collapsed after the 800 metres, thereby enabling male and female critics of women's sport to underline feminine fragility. As late as 1949 the President of the International Olympic Committee, Avery Brundage, said: 'I think women's events should be confined to those appropriate for women – swimming, tennis, figure skating and fencing, but certainly not shot-putting.'

Attempts were still being made to eliminate the shot-put and discus from the women's events in 1966. Today, women are still excluded from the hammer, pole-vault, triple-jump and modern pentathlon. Traditional ideas of which sports are appropriate for women remain powerful. Perhaps this is not surprising in a sporting world in which the main organisations are run by men: there was not one woman on the International Olympic Committee until 1981.

Additional pressures for women: this article on world-class javelin thrower, Tessa Sanderson, was written in 1975. Her male counterparts were judged solely on their athletic ability but female athletes also had to conform to notions of femininity. How far have attitudes changed today?

Tessa Sanderson: young, gifted, and black... and liberated

Back in the days even before she became a world-class javelin thrower, Tessa Sanderson struck us as the epitome of a gracefully sporting young lady.

by John Hopkins

Searching for a liberated sportswoman in International Women's Year, we came across friendly, sexy, bubbly and pretty Tessa Sanderson, an outstanding athlete, a natural games player and a liberated young lady. Swimming begins her week and dancing in Birmingham, Wolverhampton or Stafford ends it. In between she squeezes in athletics training, swimming, dancing – and work.

Tessa was born in Jamaica 19 years ago and now lives in Wednesfield, Wolverhampton. For most of her life she has enjoyed sport. 'At school I hardly bothered with lessons, specially maths,' she says. 'But I always looked forward to games.'

When sportswomen do compete, they have to face a question which sportsmen do not. Do they conform to accepted notions of what is feminine? They have to look right, as well as play well.

It is ironic that in Britain anxieties about spectator behaviour at the national game of football has produced calls from some quarters that more women should be encouraged to attend matches.

Would sport generally benefit from an influx of female ideas? Or would the masculine values which have been at the core of all sport mean that women in sport, in most roles, have to behave like men to be accepted and successful?

The joy of sport

However, there is another side to sport which helps to explain its hold on so many people in so many countries. These people would agree that 'The rhythms of sport, the sensations, and the emotions, are often the most intense and pleasurable ever experienced'. Such feelings also seem to be universal. Great games, great players, great championship seasons, as one writer said, 'lie cool and sweet in the memory for ever'.

The joy of sport is real enough for those who play at the top level, for those who once played at the very bottom level or for those who simply watch. And these joys are accessible to all – from young Bengalis in Calcutta, to middle-aged Japanese, American blue-collar workers and African intellectuals. A love of a particular sport, or team, or player, often lasts a lifetime. Loyalty to British football clubs, for example, is remarkable. In spite of recent commercial disasters, few have been allowed to collapse and disappear. It is part of a feeling that some things are beyond money. Supporters often feel their club belongs to them, even though they clearly do not own it.

Young black footballers at Crossroads, Capetown, in South Africa. The enjoyment of sport should be accessible to all – for life.

Powerful and long-lasting football loyalties are not unique to Britain. In 1985, a wealthy Brazilian left $360 million to the Bangu Football Club of Rio. In origin they were a factory team, and most of their supporters came from a working-class district: the Zona Norte. He had supported them from boyhood. As he grew rich, he could have changed his allegiance to the fashionable Fluminense club, the team of the wealthy, but he did not.

Even the professional players, hard-bitten and cynical though many of them are, often love their sport more than anything else in life. There is nothing they can do so well and it is sometimes tragic that some feel that their life is over when they can do it no longer. But their skill, practice and determination has brought many of them memorable moments which they will recall with pleasure throughout the rest of their lives. In 1951 the Brooklyn Dodgers and the New York Giants played off for baseball's National League title. In the last inning of the third and final game, with the Giants losing by two runs and in an apparently hopeless position, Bobby Thompson came to bat with two men on base and hit the most famous home run in baseball history. This is how he later recalled it: ·

To this day, I can never adequately describe the feeling that went through me as I circled the bases ... I can remember feeling as if time were just frozen. It was a delirious, delicious moment and when my feet finally touched homeplate and I saw my team-mates' faces that's when I realised I had won the pennant with one swing of the bat. And I'd be a liar if I didn't admit that I'll cherish that moment till the day I die.

L. Heiman, D. Weiner, B. Gutman, *When the Cheering Stops: Former Major Leaguers talk about their Game and their Lives*, 1990.

Sport cannot save the world but it can help to make it a better place. Those people who love it, either from the inside or the outside, have to be prepared, though, to see that standards of conduct are not allowed to slip in the pursuit of success. Sport is part of society and must imitate life. It may reflect bad feelings between individuals or groups. It may, as we have seen, reinforce them. It can hardly be their cause. On the other hand, sport can stimulate generosity of spirit and friendship. But as in every other walk of life, sports enthusiasts will have to seek actively for the best and challenge the shabby and dishonest. As in so many social activities there are optimists and pessimists on the value of sport. An anonymous wit once said that a pessimist was just a well-informed optimist. It is the hope of this writer that after confronting the issues raised in this book the reader is better placed to assess sport's place in the modern world.

Only a game: the philosophy of sportsmanship, as discussed at a primary school in Yorkshire.

Ian: "I play to win. Sometimes I get mad and tell t'ref off. Teacher, Mrs Clarke, says: 'Shut up and get on with t' game.'"

Debbie: "Arguing is stupid! If you don't think it's right, well you can try again!"

Ian: "Not if it's last match."

Debbie: "You can win the cup next year."

Ian: "Not if it's a better team the next year you can't."

Debbie: "Yes you can. Your team might be better itself. Anyway you can't win by blaming the ref."

Ian: "Sometimes you can. If the ref's one of our players, you get him to let you score. If he's one of theirs, they do the same."

Debbie: "That's just cheating!"

Ian: "It's not."

Debbie: "That's just cheating!"

Ian: "What about rounders, then? There are no referees in that, so you can cheat if you want."

Debbie: "We don't . . . Cheats shouldn't play."

FURTHER RESOURCES

Introductory Books

Tony Mason, Sport in Britain *(Faber & Faber 1988)*

Sebastian Coe, David Teasdale, David Wickham, More Than a Game *(BBC 1992)*

More Advanced Studies

History

Allen Guttmann, Women's Sports. A History *(Columbia University Press, New York 1991)*

Eric Halliday, Rowing in England. A Social History *(MUP 1990)*

Richard Holt, Sport and the British *(OUP 1989)*

Simon Inglis, The Football Grounds of England and Wales *(Collins-Willow 1983)*

Tony Mason, Sport in Britain. A Social History *(CUP 1989)*

Wray Vamplew, The Turf. A Social and Economic History of Horse Racing *(Allen Lane 1976)*

Gareth Williams and Dai Smith, Fields of Praise. The Official History of the Welsh Rugby Union *(University of Wales 1980)*

The Contemporary Scene

John Bale, The Brawn Drain. Foreign Student Athletes in American Universities *(University of Illinois 1990)*

Ernest Cashmore, Making Sense of Sport *(Routledge 1990)*

Ernest Cashmore, Black Sportsman *(RKP 1982)*

R. Espy, The Politics of the Olympic Games *(University of California Press, Berkeley 1979)*

Barrie Houlihan, The Government and Politics of Sport *(Routledge 1991)*

P. McIntosh, Fair Play: Ethics in Sport and Education *(Heinemann 1979)*

Henry Solomon, The Exercise Myth *(Angus & Robertson 1985)*

John Williams and Stephen Wagg (eds), British football and social change *(Leicester University Press 1991)*

Sports Science

Peter G. Bursztyn, Physiology for Sports People. A Serious users guide to the body *(MUP 1990)*

T. Donohoe and N. Johnson, Foul Play: drug abuse in sports *(Blackwell 1986)*

E. Grayson, Sport and the Law *(Butterworth 1988)*

Karon Inge and Peter Brukener, Food for Sport *(Heinemann, Australia 1986)*

Anne de Cooy, Food for Action *(Pelham 1987)*

D.R. Mottram, Drugs in Sport *(Spon 1988)*

John Syer and Christopher Connolly, Sporting Body, Sporting Mind. An Athlete's Guide to Mental Training *(CUP 1984)*

Steve Wootton, Nutrition for Sport *(Simon Schuster 1988)*

Peter Terry, The Winning Mind *(Thorsons 1989)*

Other Countries

Arthur Ashe, A Hard Road to Glory: A History of the African-American Athlete, *3 Vols (Warner Books, New York 1988)*

J. J. Coakley, Sport in Society: Issues and Controversies *(Times Mirror/Mosley College Publishing St Louis 1986)*

Allen Guttmann, From Ritual to Record *(Columbia University Press 1978)*

Ann Hall, Trevor Slack, Garry Smith, David Whitson, Sport in Canadian Society *(McClelland and Stewart, Toronto 1991)*

P.M. Hoose, Necessities: Racial Barriers in American Sport *(Random House, New York 1989)*

C.L.R. James, Beyond the Boundary *(Stanley Paul 1963)*

Jim McKay, No Pain, No Gain? Sport and Australian Culture *(Prentice Hall, Australia 1991)*

Brian Stoddart, Saturday Afternoon Fever. Sport in the Australian Culture *(Angus Robertson, Australia 1986).*

Organisations Providing Information

British Olympic Association, 1 Wandsworth Plain, London, SW18 1EH

Central Council of Physical Recreation, Francis House, Francis Street, London, SW1P 1DE

Football Trust, Walkden House, 10 Melton Street, London, NW1 2EJ

National Coaching Foundation, 4 College Close, Beckett Park, Leeds, LS6 3QH

National Playing Fields Association, 25 Ovington Square, London, SW13 1LQ

Sports Council, 16 Upper Woburn Place, London, WC1H 0QP

Sports Documentation Centre, University of Birmingham, University Library, Birmingham B15 2TT

Sports Pages Bookshop, Caxton Walk, 94–96 Charing Cross Road, London, WC2H 0JG

Index